THE
$150,000
MUSIC DEGREE

Rick Barker
Wade Sutton

❧ TABLE OF CONTENTS

✖ ABOUT THE AUTHORS

Rick Barker, Music Industry Blueprint (Rick@RickBarker.com)

Rick Barker is looked upon as one of the music industry's best marketers and artist developers, having spent two years managing the day-to-day operations of superstar Taylor Swift. He also created the "Nashville To You" radio tour, which played a role in the early development of several acts, such as Little Big Town and Sugarland.

Barker's impact on music extends to the industry's record labels. He was the first record promoter hired by Big Machine's Scott Borchetta, where he had a role in the label's first Number One record with singer-songwriter Jack Ingram. Barker later founded his own marketing and consulting firm, at which his first client was Sony Music Nashville.

He is also the mastermind behind the Music Industry Blueprint, a development service now teaching artists from around the world everything they need to know about the complicated music business. His marketing strategies have since been featured in a number of publications, including Billboard Magazine.

Wade Sutton, Rocket to the Stars (WadeSutton@RockettotheStars.com)

Rocket to the Stars creator and director Wade Sutton spent nearly two decades working as a radio journalist before founding one of the largest artist development competitions in the Eastern United States in 2010.

Since creating Rocket to the Stars, Wade has worked to help singers and bands around the world by teaching them how to better interact with the media and fans, helping them prepare for interviews, writing artist biographies and press releases, and assisting in the creation of their electronic press kits. He also serves as a live music producer, helping artists make their live performances more entertaining, resulting in those clients making more fans, increasing their e-mail subscriptions, and making more money.

His articles on artist development have been read by people in more than twenty countries and have been shared by top music industry officials and voice instructors, marketing experts, radio stations, and bands. Wade is also a contributor to several websites, including Music Clout.

✄ FORWARD

Danger and Opportunity

John Dwinell, Daredevil Production

Baron Rothschild, an 18th century British nobleman and member of the Rothschild banking family, is credited with saying, "The time to buy is when there's blood in the streets." I'm quite sure, since you have your hands on this book that you must be aware that the music business is in a serious crisis; yes, there is blood in the streets. Did you know the Chinese word for crisis is made up of two characters meaning danger and opportunity.

That is the way I think about the music business; danger and opportunity. The old music business required you to make demos and connections until you could find a label that was willing to sign you, invest at least $1,000,000.00, and even then you had to get really lucky again to end up in the 10% of signed artists that actually made money. You heard me right. In the hay day of the music business, only 10% of the artists made money, meaning 90% of the signed artists LOST money.

The old music industry business model was beholden to what they call the Tyranny of Space. There was a finite amount of valuable shelf space on which to place your CD and an even more finite amount of radio spins allotted for new artists. The old business model created situations where an artist who had a great record was charting in the Top 20 on Billboard, touring like crazy, creating real momentum, essentially doing EVERYTHING right, but

7

would often lose their deal because the label found another act in the same genre with a little more momentum and had to drop the prior artist due to the Tyranny of Space.

Huh?

Yeah man, there are only so many radio spins so the label would (intelligently) put their eggs into the better basket. THIS is the old model that is falling apart right before our eyes. Tragic to some, I am quite sure, but very necessary and much better overall for the art and the artists who create it. As an artist you have to be aware of the big picture to really see the opportunities that lie within the danger and chaos.

The new music business doesn't suffer from the Tyranny of Space. The costs to make a record are much less expensive, there are no distribution issues because there is always room for one more CD on a server, and (most) social media is free. So, for an artist, the velvet ropes are gone and the luck of the draw has disappeared to a large degree.

As an artist, YOU now hold all the power to write music that YOU love, record it the way YOU want, to find YOUR audience online, and sell YOUR music.

As an artist, YOU now have the opportunity to create a small profitable business that will sustain YOU and your family while doing what YOU were born to do; music.

As an artist, YOU now hold all the power to create your reality and prove to the world that there is a market for your specific music. Once YOU do that work, all the big money in the form of private investors and major record labels will find YOU.

As an artist, YOU literally can change what mainstream popular music is going to sound like.

Don't believe me? Look at the Zac Brown Band and Florida-Georgia Line. Whether you like these artists or not, they got deals after they created the buzz and sales on their own. This was after every label turned down both acts.

So how do you do it?

You have to start by understanding that the new music business now suffers from an equally abrasive oppression called the Tyranny of Choice. Have you ever eaten at a restaurant (like Jerry's Famous Deli in L.A.) with a ridiculously massive menu?? I was always apprehensive to eat at JFD because I could never decide what to eat! There were too many choices.

This is the current issue we need to overcome as artists, managers, labels, etc.: How do you stand out? How do you rise above the noise on the radar screen?

The answer is 10% making good music and 90% doing good business.

If you are reading these words, you are a musician looking for answers as to how you can take the next step with your musical aspirations. You are searching for the right formula that will allow you to make a living, maybe get a record deal, tour, improve as a writer, improve your live show, find and communicate to your future fans, etc. And, whether you like it or not, you ARE also a small business person and entrepreneur (doesn't that sound sexy?).

As a small business person I have found certain Mastermind Groups to be invaluable over the years. In Napoleon Hill's Think and Grow Rich, a mastermind group was defined as the coordination of knowledge and effort of two or more people, who work toward a definite purpose, in the spirit of harmony. At Daredevil Production, LLC, my business partner, Kelly Schoenfeld, and I are constantly searching to expand our mastermind group. Our business model is to occupy the vacuum that exists in the new music business with regards to developing talent artistically as well as the ever-so-crucial market development (which is fancy talk for sales and exposure). As this new music business is a constantly moving target, it is MISSION CRITICAL to us that our mastermind group consist of trusted experts with forward thinking mentalities in the NEW music business (Music Row is rich with successful old school thinkers who are too busy, stubborn, or stupid to embrace the new model for success) and that these people have fresh ideas. You see, the old ways of marketing music and developing brands are quickly dying.

Kelly and I are very blessed and proud to have two such gentlemen in our mastermind group; Rick Barker and Wade Sutton.

I became aware of Rick Barker when I received an email with a subject line that said, I Loved Your Blog and the opening line was, "why haven't we met?" We became fast friends, as Rick was from the Mother Ship with regards to the concepts and strategies we believed were going to lead the new emerging artists into sustainable careers. Rick's brain blows me away. Kelly laughs at me because I LOVE to talk but, whenever Rick is talking, I shut up. I'm fascinated when Rick gets weird about marketing artists. One could surmise that, with Rick, (who used to manage Taylor Swift) the readers of this book will get a $150,000 music education if they chose. After all, hindsight is always 20/20. There is a popular idiom that states, those who can, can. Those who can't, teach. Rick does both. Half of his book is made up of transcripts of Rick's YouTube series, 25 Minutes to Nashville where he answers questions, discusses concepts, and offers amazing guidance about how to grow your business as an artist. Rick makes these videos during his daily commute to work on Music Row. What a gift! SAE believes so much in what Rick teaches, that the school has incorporated his Music Industry Blueprint concepts into its own Music Business curriculum. I have learned so much from him during our relationship and I know you will too.

I became aware of Wade Sutton through our Twitter account (and Rick as well, if my memory serves me correctly). I have had the pleasure of several lengthy phone conversations with Wade. Again, I learned so much! Wade's vast experience in radio and media is astounding. As Daredevil Production, LLC puts together the necessary pieces for our upcoming record label, I realize that Wade will be invaluable. We lack knowledge in the PR components, understanding media relations, and mission critical area of simply rising above the din of every indie label/indie band/ indie artist's attempt for attention. And I resonate profoundly with Wade's no-nonsense approach. I LOVED the chapter in this book called "Why Bands Need to Stop Bitching About Venues" because I would have written it with the same tone.

Bottom line is everybody can always improve. To be a successful business (which you have to be to succeed as an artist these days, like it or not) you need a good team, accurate information, and the drive to execute many little tasks that are crucial to your momentum. This book contains many of the concepts you need to take your artistry to the next level.

Listen, it's one thing to read this book. The difference between being a book owner and making a living doing something you love lies within these pages and the content on Wade and Rick's respective websites.

You can grow your brand.
You can grow your audience.
You can expand your influence.
You can make a living making music.

Doesn't that mean you're successful?

CHAPTER 1

The Approach You Need

Why a Career in Music Requires a Leap of Faith

Wade Sutton, Rocket to the Stars

If you want to make music your full-time career, you will eventually have to take a deep breath and either jump from the cliff or wait for somebody to give you a push.

I'm speaking from personal experience.

I created Rocket to the Stars and built it up while maintaining a full-time job in radio news. Small market radio does not pay very well but I loved what I did. I was only 20-years-old when I was promoted to news director at the first radio station I worked for.

I have covered high profile homicide trials and sat inches away from convicted child killers. On the day of the September 11th attacks, my co-worker and I were the first two people in the United States to interview by phone nationally syndicated talk show host Michael Gallagher minutes after he was forced to evacuate the Empire State Building.

I have been on the sidelines and in the locker rooms during NFL games. I have been back stage at concerts. I covered nearly forty elections. When a child in our community shot and killed his father's pregnant girlfriend, I found myself covering the story for a number of radio stations, some as far away as Ireland.

Then, after 18 years of doing news in my hometown, I was called into a manager's office and was told my position was being eliminated due to budget problems. It was 10:40 on a Friday morning. There had been no indication to me that my job was in danger. Sitting there blindsided by the news, the only thing going through my mind was figuring out how I was going to support my seven-year-old daughter. I had been living a normal life with a normal job and a normal daily routine while collecting a normal pay check. My "normal" had been destroyed as if somebody had tossed a hand grenade at it.

I walked into my office and packed my personal belongings, including a Mr. Potato Head my daughter made nearly four years before. I said farewell to people who had been like family for almost half my life. I was an emotional wreck.

But it was during the drive home that I stopped being upset. After spending four years growing and developing Rocket to the Stars, I realized NOW was the time to make this my career. I saw that this was my opportunity to stop making money for other people and to start making it for myself. I understood that my knowledge and creativity could now be used to dictate how far I went instead of being held back by people destined to forever tread the waters of middle management.

Do I have the safety net of a "normal job paycheck"? Of course not. And that is some scary shit when you are a single parent not receiving any financial assistance from an ex-spouse. In losing my job, I was pushed from the aforementioned cliff. I was forced to face a lot of fears. And so will you if you really want to have a successful music career.

You will work harder than you ever thought possible...

I start working as soon as my daughter gets on the school bus at 7:30 am. I do not stop until she comes home and, some days, deadlines force me to have to do some work when she is home. It isn't out of the ordinary that I find myself continuing to work after she goes to bed.

Your full-time career in music will never be forty hours a week. You sure as hell won't have weekends off. If you are looking for a life that is more leisurely than a "regular job", you should look elsewhere. When shit needs done, you need to do it or it will just sit there. Your level of success will be connected directly to your productivity, decision-making, and luck.

Your standard of "working hard" will change forever. It will change whom you want to surround yourself with and will make you think twice about working with many of the people already close to you.

You will up your game...or you will fail.

You will spend more time working on your business than your product...

Is the grunt work that goes into promoting, booking shows, communicating with fans on social media, and updating your website not glamorous enough to hold your interest? Then you better find a way to pay somebody with those skills to do it for you.

That time you spend on stage performing for fans and having the lights on you is only a small fraction of what goes on when you are doing music on a full-time basis. And don't even get me started on things like selling sponsorships, accounting, keeping the channels of communication open with the media, and many other things that need to be done.

One of the hardest things for me with Rocket to the Stars is finding the correct balance between promoting, creating new content for the website, and providing services to clients in the form of consultations, training, web designing, and writing for them. And now I am preparing for the possibility of taking on additional teaching gigs. The day has only 24 hours.

You will be afraid... but it will be liberating...

Facing the possibility of failing at something you love doing holds a lot of people back from ever trying. It is amazing the number of excuses people come up with to not try. That subject matter was discussed recently on a podcast hosted by two people I know: Billy Grisak and Bob Baker. They called it the "Big Buts", referring to how people always say they want to pursue something but then come up with empty reasons to not do it.

Afraid you won't have money to put food on the table? Believe me when I say that is an excellent motivator to get your ass moving. Worried about health insurance? Work hard enough to bring in the money to buy it. Scared you might have to pick up and move to another city to give yourself a better chance at succeeding? Shut up and pack your shit.

I recently wrote a biography for a singer who used to be AMISH! She loved music so much and wanted to do it so badly; she risked being excommunicated by her family and friends by leaving the sect to pursue music. She earned her driver's license and packed her belongings into one bag and left. Now she is married, taking voice lessons, is performing with a band, writing her own songs, and is planning to move to Nashville. She didn't make any excuses. Neither should you.

And if you do end up failing, so what? Seriously, what is the big deal? The sun will come up tomorrow and life will go on. Would you rather live with the regret of wondering what could have been? Regrets suck. Besides, think about the example you would be setting for your own kids. Would you rather they be too scared to chase their own dreams?

You will find out who your friends are...

You will spend so much time working on your music and your business that you won't have anything else to talk about with your non-musician friends. In fact, they will probably get sick and tired of hearing you talk about it. Your real friends won't care and will continue to pull for you.

You will also find out the hard way that some people claiming to be your friends really aren't. This will definitely happen as you start to experience more and more success. It can be even worse for artists still in high school or college. Do not allow their jealousy to bring you down or hold you back. People like that will have a difficult time succeeding in life and will oftentimes latch on to others who are succeeding and try to keep those people at their own level. Sadly, a lot of them don't even realize they are doing it. You don't need people like that in your life. Don't be the one who hits the brakes on the music career to keep a "friend" around.

Even if they support your decision, your family likely won't understand you...

Once you start to survive in a world in which you operate your own business, music included, you will find yourself looking at things much differently from people working a regular job. That includes your family, some of whom will support you, while others will not. They will ask questions and raise concerns. You will probably answer a lot of the same questions over and over.

They will be living in a different world than you. Most people are conditioned to get up in the morning, go to work and punch in, put in their eight hours, punch out and go home. Doing something that breaks that mold is foreign to them. You will live a very unhappy life if you make your career choices based upon the limitations of somebody else's knowledge.

I'll leave you with a post I made on Facebook a day or two after losing my job at the radio stations: "Sometimes you jump. Sometimes you get pushed. Either way, you are going to learn to fly."

Do Not Make These Mistakes

Rick Barker, Music Industry Blueprint's
"25 Minutes From Nashville"

We are going to talk about first impressions. Acting like you belong, not geeking out in front of the industry people or famous people, and making that first impression. We are going to cover a lot of ground and the reason is that, this week here in Nashville, is what's called CRS Week. It's Country Radio Seminar and it's where all the major important players in the radio world come to Nashville and the labels are showcasing new artists. They are really trying to show you what they've got coming out and what they are working on.

It's a chance for all the big superstars to say "thank you" to radio for all of their support. There are some great panels and some great discussions. I don't want to say "anybody who's anybody," but the people who can make a difference in your life are here this week. And it is a feeding frenzy with independent artists who, without knowing it and who are being given bad advice, can do major damage to their career before their career even gets started.

I want to give you some hints and advice and then I also want to talk about one of my Music Industry Blueprint members, Brittany Bexton. Brittany was contacted and has interviewed a couple of times with an independent label who's interested in working with her. Whenever someone calls and asks me about anything, one of the first things I do, if not the first, is I go online to see what their online impression looks like. If they don't come across professional online, which is for the whole world to see, that's a tell-tell sign of what's to come. If they don't take the responsibility of looking professional and up-to-date for their own product, why are they going to do that for your product?

So, let's start with CRS and some of the "do's" and "do not's". First off, leave your CDs and your music at home. They did not come here to discover you; they came here to build relationships and further the relationships that they have. Are they interested in making new relationships? Absolutely, but only with people that act like they belong.

You could be sitting downstairs at the Renaissance Hotel and hand somebody a CD and I guarantee you, 99.9% of the time, that CD never even makes it back to the room. It ends up in the trash, not because they think it might not be the best CD they've ever heard. That's just not why they are there and most of them aren't going to sit around. Most of them are drunk by the way, I mean; it's a big drunk fest here at CRS. A lot of people go hang out at what's called the Bridge Bar just to try to get some contact with somebody that might be able to help them and half the time they won't even remember the conversation.

So don't hand out CDs. Everyone's going to have a nametag on. Write down their name when you get a chance, go follow them on Twitter and like them on Facebook. Most of these people have social media sites that you can use to follow-up and connect with them there; it goes back to building that relationship first. Also, two, if you see a label person don't geek out. Just act like you belong, you know, their name's on and you go, "Hey Scott, how are you doing?"Just act like you know them. They meet everybody so they are just going to go, "Hey, how are you?" Half the time they won't go, "I don't know who you are? Who are you?" No! They will nod and go right along.

It goes a long way, especially if they are standing with maybe a big program director of a radio station. You show proper etiquette. You act like you belong. You don't geek out. Also, if you are an independent artist or you manage an independent artist, do not stand downstairs looking like a hoe. I have no other way to say it. There have been some crazy folks down there and you know, their manager is sitting over there and the manager is doing all the talking. Unless your manager knows a bunch of people and can introduce you to a bunch of people, leave him behind.

You go and scope it out. If you see other artists and you walk across and you see it's Tim McGraw just say, you know, "Hey Tim. How are you?" That's it. Don't go, "Oh my God. I am your biggest fan. Oh my God. I would love to open for you. Oh, here's my music video. Would you listen to my music?" No, they won't listen to your music so don't waste that time. Act like you belong because that's what you should be doing in life. I remember when I used to try to sneak in to clubs when I was younger and we used to say, "If you act like you belong, you belong."

"If you want to be a star one day, act like a star. If you want to be equals with them, act like you are equals with them now. So that's just kind of a little CRS tid-bit there. A lot of people don't even get the chance to listen to CDs anymore. As a matter of fact my CD player doesn't even work. It's got four CDs in it that I can't get out.

When somebody says, "Hey, I am in the music business. Would you check out my stuff?" The first thing I ask them, and I am training other people to do, is "what's your website?" And then when I get to your website, please, do not make it hard for me to hear your music. If your music is not on the front page, make sure that there is at least a button that sends me to where I can hear it. Don't give me samples. Give me the whole thing. What are you holding back for? What are you teasing for?

There are too many places and choices for me to go listen to music. What am I going to do, spend a day listening to samples? No, I want to enjoy the song. I want to get to the bridge. I want to hear everything you have to offer. If you've gotten my attention and I've gotten to that place where I can listen to your music that may be the only chance you will ever get to share your music with me, you better give me all of it. And that may be the only chance you have to show me what you look like in a video and it may be the only chance you get to show me what's going on with your social media sites. So make sure that they are rock solid before you start inviting people there. And don't go and say, "Well, Rick, I didn't invite you there. You asked me for the information, ta-da!"

So before you get yourself prepared, don't go out and start advertising to me that you are an artist because when you tell me, "Hey, I'm an artist" what you're telling me is "I am ready to compete with Taylor and Carrie and Tim and Rascal Flatts and Bruno Mars and everyone else." Because that's what you are saying when you walk into a radio station. And that's whom you are competing with. You are competing for airtime with those artists so, if you want to be considered in the same breath as those artists, the easiest thing you can do is compete with them online. As far as your presentation goes, you can look like a major-label rock star. That's up to you. Just make sure you have the right people teaching you how to do that.

The next thing I want to talk about is an independent record label. There are some amazing people out there wanting to try and help make differences in the lives of independent artists and I applaud them. What happens when I get a call from an artist and he says, "Hey, have you heard of this company?" What's the first thing I do? You got it! I go to their website and if their website looks like it was built in 1991, I usually tell the artist, "I don't know if this is the right label for you because I don't know if they can compete in today's music business." I don't say that to be mean. I told Brittany earlier, I said, "Look, they never had a hit but it doesn't mean that you can't be their first.". There always has to be a first for something, you know what I am saying? There's always a first something. Why shouldn't that first be you? What you want to make sure is that they have the resources in place in order to help get you there or, if they don't, do they have an exit plan where you can get out of your deal and maybe partner with a label. Find out what their buy-out is.

Make sure that you have the funding and the resources in place to be able to compete at a major level because, whether you are an independent or a major, it still costs the same. If the majors aren't taking shortcuts with their product, you can't take short cuts... If it takes a record label with a full staff, years of experience, years of relationships, $500,000 to break an artist, it's probably going to take you a million because you don't have their years of experience or their relationships.

People who try to do it inexpensively sometimes end up coming across as an inexpensive product. You do not want to be an inexpensive product. With the tools that are available today, you can look like a rock star, you can deliver quality, and you can do it at an affordable price. I don't think everything the labels spend money on should be spent. So, yeah, there is a way to compete in there. You've just got to make sure that you have someone that's helping guide you in that direction.

CHAPTER 2

The Importance of Development

Are We Giving Artists the Right Tools to Succeed?

Rick Barker, Music Industry Blueprint's
"25 Minutes From Nashville"

I was talking with a client yesterday and it's almost like some of the things that I showed them were these big revelations. It's like, "Wow! If I would have only known this, or if someone would have just shown me this before we had invested all this money." And it got me thinking that being an artist is one of the only jobs where we just throw unqualified people out to work and just expect them to succeed. In almost every other job there is some form of training. Athletes have coaches. They have training. They have a lot of different things that teach them how to be and do that job. What we have are vocal lessons, media trainings, performances, and we teach them how to play instruments, but there is no one really teaching artists how to be artists. We get upset when they get out there and they can't figure it out on their own when they are on radio tour, or they are already out on a major tour and it doesn't work out. That is one of the major reasons why I started the Music Industry Blueprint in the first place, is to teach artist development.

When I was out with Taylor, I loved the marketing, I loved the teaching, I loved getting creative, and I loved finding ways to get audiences to spend more money than they were prepared to spend when they got to a show. The thing that I didn't like is I hated dealing with the label stuff, I hated dealing with the paperwork, and I hated dealing with the bus drivers and the bands. That wasn't my strength. So instead of staying in a position and staying in a job that I wasn't happy in and I couldn't be effective in, I went ahead and created my own company where I could teach artists how to be artists. A lot of people don't like doing it. I love doing it and I'm having a blast teaching it.

We don't expect doctors to know everything, the advanced specialists even go to more school. So what could we be doing to better prepare artists before they go on radio tour, before they go to a studio, before they get dropped into the limelight where we want to build them up and knock them down? What can we do as an industry to better prepare our artists for this journey? As a matter of fact, we need to think about it pretty hard because we're funding it. The industry is funding their development but the development is happening at the wrong time. It needs to happen before the product has been recorded or at least while the product is being recorded.

There are four pillars to any successful business. And we have to start looking at the artist as a business.

1. Brand
2. Build
3. Cultivate
4. Sell

Who are you? What are you? Is there a market for what it is that you have? Build an audience. Then we need to nurture that audience.

We need to build a relationship. We got really good at building this huge database but then we didn't realize that people don't like to be sold every single moment of every single day in every single email and we blew through those databases. That's why the open rates are so low and you can't get anybody to hear your message. Then you go sell.

Most people just record a record then go into sell mode and wonder why it didn't sell or they just get an artist and take some pictures or shoot a video, record some music and they put them out in the marketplace then wonder why they don't sell. Well it's because the two middle parts are what is very important. It's the two middle parts, the building of the audience and the cultivating of the audience, which actually determines the sell. What we teach in the Music Industry Blueprint is to really start engaging your fan base on a daily basis. We teach how to segment your list and why that's important. What I mean by that is not every single person gets every single message. Not every single person who is on your list is there for the same reasons so why would you market to all of them the same way?

That's one of the things that we are really focusing on right now. I call it the three levels of fandom. The fans go through these stages. There's that person who just happens to see you on Twitter and thought you're good looking, liked you and maybe decided they would sign up for your list and they did. Then there's that person that maybe follows you on Facebook and Twitter. You leave a post; they comment every now and then, they tell their friends about you. There's that second level of fandom. They're a little bit more engaged.

And then there's that fan that listens to everything you do and say, buys everything you sell and goes to every show you have. That's your SUPERFAN. That's that level of fandom that we want them all to get to. Those are the people that we need to create more opportunities for and to really be engaged with because they are the ones that will change your life, they are the ones that will move the needle for you. So we cannot communicate with them the same way we do to the casual fan. We can't continue to teach the artist to just go out and sing their heart out. We need to get them out there and make sure they're staying engaged on a daily basis. One of the things that we need to do is to make sure that we are properly training their team. A lot of times their team can completely sabotage them without knowing all the efforts that you as the label or somebody like myself is putting in place, if we don't take the time to make sure that they're trained properly.

Why You Need a Live Music Producer (and Don't Even Know It)

Wade Sutton, Rocket to the Stars

"The vast majority of income for most bands is brought in by their live shows, yet most of them spend little or no time trying to make those live shows more entertaining for their audiences."

That is a quote I scribbled in my notebook nearly five months prior to me writing this article. I was in Nashville for the annual Tom Jackson Boot Camp, a two-day crash course in live performance instruction, music promotion, and networking. Tom, considered by many to be the best live music producer in the world (and a very good friend to Rocket to the Stars), was talking about the manner in which many bands and performers prioritize their time and energy when it comes to rehearsing for their shows.

Here is the thing: Many people SERIOUSLY pursuing music as a career, mostly those in cities like Nashville and Los Angeles, understand what a live music producer brings to the table. I'm talking about performers actively pursuing development and doing everything they can to improve at their craft. But a lot of artists outside that specific group don't even know what a live music producer does, let alone works with one.

And that is a big part of the reason why so many artists are having such a difficult time standing out from the crowd...

Meet Tom Jackson...

Live music producer Tom Jackson has worked with some of the biggest names in the music industry, including Taylor Swift, The Band Perry, Jordin Sparks, and more! He travels the world instructing singers and bands on how to improve their live shows so they are more entertaining for audiences. He has spoken at representative events at Berklee College of Music, the Noise Music Conference in New Zealand, and Canadian Music Week in Toronto. Tom is also the author of "Live Music Method" and creator of the "All Roads Lead to the Stage" DVD series.

So, what does a live music producer do?

"A live music producer takes an artist and develops who they are on stage," said Tom. "They help the artist find 'moments' in their songs that are memorable, and help them deliver them visually in a way that their audiences understand."

The term "moment" is extremely important when it comes to live music production. Think of them as specific things that happen during a live show that leave such an impression on audiences that fans remember and talk about them years later. When everybody attending a Garth Brooks concert sings "Unanswered Prayers" and Garth acts surprised even though it happens at every concert? That is an "emotional moment." When pyrotechnics are shooting from Gene Simmons' guitar and fake blood is pouring from his mouth during a KISS concert? That is a "visual moment." That time when your favorite band took your favorite four-minute song and turned it into an unexpected 12-minute ear orgasm that could never be played on the radio? Yea, that is a "musical moment." They are planned meticulously and then strategically placed at certain points of a live show for maximum emotional effect.

"Moments are when an audience gets so quiet you can hear a pin drop or when you do something that creates a standing ovation or your audience is brought to tears," Tom added.

Simply put, these things don't happen by accident... even when they appear to be entirely spontaneous on stage.

Why invest in a live music producer?

We were only a few minutes into our interview when I came at Tom with a question I know many artists ask when live music production is brought up: In terms of expenditures and income, why should an artist shell out large sums of money to a live music producer, whether it be you or anybody else offering that service? What is the impact on a band's bottom line?

"Because creating moments during a live show results in artists selling more merchandise," he said firmly. "People who experience moments want to be able to take something home with them that allows them to relive those moments." It isn't uncommon for bands working with skilled live music producers to see increases in merchandise sales. One example Tom and I discussed had to do with a band that had been performing for a period of time.

"We went in and started working with this band on their performance skills," he explained. "About a week later their manager called and said their merchandise sales had increased by 600%. They were doing the same songs they were doing before we worked with them but now they had moments in their show. And that isn't uncommon."

So if hiring a live music producer can result in a positive return on the band's investment, why don't more bands do it?

"Because so many bands are spending their money on the wrong things," Tom told me. "There was a band I worked with that was set to perform at an expo in Canada. They had 20-thousand dollars to use and they were going to spend all of it on recording."

Their thinking at the time, Tom said, was that they would record and produce a CD that could be given out to the audience at the expo.

"But the problem was people at the expo were going to watch this band perform live and decide from that whether or not they liked them," Tom laughed. "And they want to spend all this money on these CDs? What are they going to do? Have everybody wear headphones and listen to it? This is at an expo. You have three songs to impress people with your live performance or you're gone!"

When egos become roadblocks...

Many singers and bands don't want to admit they need help with their live performances. A lot of them will say things like "I'll turn it on once I get on stage" or "But my shows are supposed to be about my music." Tom launched into another story.

"I once had a phone call from the manager of this band and he was asking me to come in and work with them," he said. "So, I'm standing in line at a Starbucks one day and these two guys are in line in front of me. I could hear them talking and I realized that one of the guys was a member of the band I was asked to train."

Tom introduced himself to the musician and told the young man that the band's manager had contacted him about helping out. When the musician asked Tom in what manner he was going to assist the band, Tom told him about the live performance training.

"He immediately took a step back and crossed his arms over his chest. He looks at me and says "But dude, our show rocks," Tom laughed. "Everybody knew the band needed this help except them. They had good songs, a record deal, and good publicity. But they were winging it on stage and it showed."

So what happened?

"About two years later I walked into that same Starbucks and there he was again. Only this time he was working behind the counter. And I really wanted to walk up to him and say "Dude...you rock!"

Rehearsing like it is a show...

Another thing a skilled live music producer does is make sure you are bringing more energy to your rehearsals. They can push you to rehearse with the same intensity needed for your live shows.

"One of the things that made Michael Jordan the greatest basketball player ever was that he was notorious for practicing so hard.

You have to go for it in rehearsal," Tom preaches. "And bands need to have that repetition."

"I remember this band I worked with that kept saying they would 'bring it' once they were in front of their audience. So I decided to film the show. We watched the tape after the show and you know what?" Tom asked. "It was no different than the rehearsal. What they were saying about turning it on at the show was nothing but a bunch of crap."

The Bribe to Subscribe: Bands and E-mails

Wade Sutton, Rocket to the Stars

It is no secret that creating and adding to a list of e-mail subscribers is one of the most important marketing tools for singers and bands.

It is also one of the most difficult and frustrating tasks to undertake.

It doesn't matter what country you are in. It doesn't matter what genre of music you perform. The benefits of being able to market directly to a fan or customer cannot be overstated. By agreeing to give you their e-mail address, a fan is essentially giving you permission to be a part of their life. That is only a fraction of the reason why getting e-mail addresses is so damn hard.

Think about it: We live in an age of loud commercials, pop-up advertisements, banner ads, naming rights being sold for pretty much everything, names of businesses plastered all over the back of event t-shirts, tickers scrolling on the bottom of television screens, and business logos on athletic uniforms. People aren't just marketed to... they are having corporate messages shoved down their throats at every minute and, unfortunately, the angst over that is trickling down to musicians trying to expand their fan bases.

So I decided it was time to get some answers. I wasn't looking for the generic suggestions you can get on any other website. Instead I wanted to roll up the sleeves and get answers from people having success at this kind of thing. And I didn't just want to know what worked. I wanted to know why so many singers and bands were failing miserably in this important part of their music careers. So I tracked down two people to help out...

Meet Rick Barker...

Rick Barker was managing recording artist Taylor Swift when her career first took off. Go back and watch videos of when she won many of her early awards and you will hear her thank him during her acceptance speeches. He spent more than a dozen years in radio before testing the waters in the recording industry, where he has made an excellent name for himself since 2004. A former consultant to Sony Music Nashville and Big Machine, he now serves as a consultant to Live Nation merchandise, offering key input on acts such as Florida Georgia Line and Brantley Gilbert. He also educates artists through his program called "Music Industry Blueprint," which teaches singers and bands how to promote themselves and create a solid foundation for their music business.

Meet Leanne Regalla...

Leanne Regalla earned a Master's Degree in International Business and now heads up two companies. One of them, Make Creativity Pay, is designed to help creative people pursue their career of choice without going broke, searching for food in dumpsters, or having to sell organs that might otherwise be needed in the future. A lot of what she does has to do with identifying possible income sources within your work and then showing clients how to market what they have to offer to people interested in their product. She also has an extensive background in music, which is at the center of her second business Livin' Out Loud Music.

What have you done for me lately?

Both the music and music marketing industries have changed a great deal over the past few years. There was a time during which artists could offer somebody a free digital download of a song and the person they were marketing themselves to would offer up their e-mail address in return. That time is long gone. Think about it: Somebody will shell out hard earned money to purchase a ticket to a show, leave their house and spend money for gas and parking, drop cash on food and drinks during the show, have a great time while they are there and then turn around and resist giving up the e-mail. Why?

"There is so much noise out there and people don't want more of it. They don't want to be e-mailed. They don't want to be marketed to. They are frankly sick of everyone wanting their e-mail addresses," says Regalla.

Barker offered up a bit of history. He explained that many potential customers became tired of e-mail marketing, not so much because they were receiving the e-mails, but more so because of what was in the e-mails.

"We saw it with bands across the country as well as the major labels. They were sending people press releases. Fans don't care about press releases. They certainly don't care when you have a show in Detroit if they live in California. The people being e-mailed were constantly being told how great a band was," Barker pointed out.

Then things started to turn ugly. With society suffering from e-mail marketing fatigue, Barker says the opt-in rates for people subscribing to e-mail lists plummeted to as low as five-percent. Since that time, everybody from the newest band to the most established label has been trying to figure out exactly what needs to be done to get somebody to type in his or her e-mail address and hit the "enter" button.

Both said something that bands should take to heart: Artists need to stop looking at e-mail as a cry for attention and start using them as a vessel for giving. Regalla calls it the "Bribe to Subscribe."

Barker refers to it as the "Ethical Bribe." Both are talking about what a band has to offer a fan to successfully get their e-mail address... and both agreed that content is king.

"I tell my clients to try to get a video of an awesome live performance of one of their songs and send that to their subscribers. Make and send them an acoustic video of a new song you are working on. Use the Internet to hold some special event that subscribers can watch and be a part of. Do an online meet-and-greet. There is so much that can be done!" she said. Regalla also points out that artists have to offer something too good to pass up.

The idea of coming up with something too good to pass up is one of the fundamental aspects of Barker's Music Industry Blueprint. He has been advising clients to offer fans seven free songs in exchange for subscribing to their e-mail lists. Barker says they have been having incredible success with the marketing plan... to the extent that some independent artists he knows are outpacing the number of subscribers to some artists currently signed to major labels. Much of it has to do with figuring out and assigning a monetary value to an individual's e-mail address.

"Bands need to start thinking. If you are a new artist, a lot of people probably weren't going to buy your CD to begin with. So you try to change their mindset so they aren't thinking they are getting seven songs because they gave you their e-mail. You present it as you wanting to give them free music but you need an e-mail address to deliver it to," Barker explained.

Committing to a comprehensive plan...

"Trying to collect e-mails is a marketing campaign that goes beyond just posting on Facebook that you want people to sign up," Regalla continues. I could almost hear a little bit of frustration in her voice when she said it. She says this is an area in which many singers and bands fail.

"They must have a comprehensive plan. Social media has opened up so many possibilities as far as marketing is concerned but you need to have a lot of things firing on all cylinders for it to work properly."

One mistake that bands make: they make a few posts on Facebook and then stop talking about it. That makes the entire process come to a screeching halt. Regalla says a lot of singers and musicians underestimate just how much work is involved and don't understand the complexities of marketing. She tells her clients they need to make a commitment to marketing their subscription sign-ups with regular postings on all forms of social media and at live shows. They key is to never stop promoting.

"Something as simple as putting a tag at the end of every video you put on YouTube telling the viewer they should visit your website and sign up. Let them know it is there. Increase the awareness so they know to go to the site."

Straight from the horse's mouth...

One of the things I like about Rick is that he goes looking for answers. During our discussion he told me about his time working with Taylor Swift and the emphasis they were putting on communicating with fans via e-mail.

"We needed to find out what it was fans wanted and what they would respond to so we went out and asked them. Everything from what information they would like to receive to how often they wanted to be contacted and many of them said they wanted to be contacted around every other week." That comment from Barker referring to the frequency of the e-mails echoed Regalla's opinion. She had commented to me just days before that people feel like the constant barrage of e-mails marketing various products is pestering them.

Barker once sent an e-mail to his own subscribers that included links to a series of videos on his own website. One of the videos discussed and showed an e-mail Swift sent to one of her subscribers. It was a personal gesture to somebody she did not know but appreciated a great deal. That kind of contact builds relationships, a vital component many bands seem to neglect these days.

"People wanted to be a part of what Taylor had going on," Barker explained. He said artists like Swift and Dave Matthews have had incredible success because they are offering things via

Internet marketing that others are not. When I pressed him for specific examples, he responded, "Tickets. Letting subscribers hear songs before they were released to the public. A lot of things. But you have to make sure it is something good before you interrupt a person's life by sending them an e-mail because that is what an e-mail is: an interruption."

"And another thing," he continued, "Musicians need to understand they are not just musicians. They are also Internet marketers. They need to stop spending three- and four-thousand dollars on EPs when they have no e-mail subscribers to market them to. It is a waste of money. They think that investing thousands of dollars into the discs means that the labels should too. It isn't happening until they have a fan base to sell to."

The tools of the trade...

When asked what e-mail collection service they would recommend to new bands, both Regalla and Barker were in agreement: MailChimp. The reason? Because MailChimp offers a free service with several great applications that bands can stick with until they reach two-thousand subscribers. Regalla points out that the free MailChimp service does not offer an auto-responder for people subscribing for the first time but Barker says he thinks bands working on a budget early on won't really need it.

Of course the question to ask is what e-mail collection services do Barker and Regalla use for their own businesses. Barker says he uses MailChimp. Regalla elected to go with AWeber, the same e-mail service we use at Rocket to the Stars. Bands wanting to go with the paid option through either company should expect to shell out around twenty dollars per month, a cost that can written off as a business expense and can be offset by monetizing the e-mails that are sent to subscribers.

Final bits of advice...

During our discussion, Barker and I spoke about ways to persuade people to subscribe to e-mail lists while attending live shows. It was brought up how a lot of bands will simply announce from the stage that attendees can visit the merchandise table to sign up. That isn't good enough.

"There are so many distractions at a live show. You can't trust people to remember what you said while you were on stage. This person will have had too much to drink. That person will be over there trying to get laid. The band needs to go to the merchandise table after the show and meet people. They have to offer ten dollars off a shirt to anybody giving their e-mail. You cover the cost of the shirt and still walk away with somebody to market to," he said. Barker also suggested bands consider setting up a number that fans can text their e-mails to during the show in exchange for a code to activate the downloads. Artists interested in doing that should consider Trumpia, which has provided mass texting services to Rocket to the Stars the past three years. Their service has been very satisfactory and they provide similar services to a number of Fortune500 companies.

Regalla had another suggestion. "Take a long term view of collecting e-mails. Don't expect one hundred e-mails the first night you are collecting them on your website. Getting e-mails is like getting fans: You get them one at a time."

CHAPTER 3

Stop Bitching (About Everything)

Quit Bitching About Record Labels

Rick Barker, Music Industry Blueprint's
"25 Minutes From Nashville"

I subscribe to a lot of blogs. I listen to a lot of people. I've been speaking all over the country. Everyone keeps bitching about the record companies. "Oh, I don't want to be signed to a major label." And, "Oh, if you sign with them, you're signing your life away and you'll never make any money."

The bottom line is this: Most of the people doing that talking, one, aren't good enough to be on a major label, and, two, they don't understand the workings of a major label. Because they never have worked for a major label, or they've never managed an artist at a major label to understand that a label could be your friend. If you've got the right product and you're the right artist, a label can absolutely change your life.

Now, is a record deal for everyone? Absolutely not. Have we heard reports of people who've signed bad record deals? Sure. Blame your attorney if you sign a bad record deal. Or don't sign it. You've got the choice.

But the thing is, right now, too many uneducated folks are talking way too much crap. So, I wanted to set the record straight. Let me say that these are my opinions and my opinions only. I have not only worked for a record label, I have managed an artist who was on a label, not major at the time I was managing her but, boy that record label sure is major now thanks to her help. And I consult major record labels. So I'm very familiar with the inner workings.

A lot of what I'm going to say is not going to be politically correct for a lot of people and, for that, I apologize. You can turn this off at any time. You can unsubscribe. You can un-follow.

I always make this preface whenever I'm speaking with anyone. Two things. One, I'm like sushi; I'm an acquired taste. I'm not for everyone. Two, my grammar absolutely sucks, but you'll completely get the point.

The record labels have the ability to take somebody from something small to outside the stratosphere. They also have the ability to totally screw things up depending on the record label and depending on the company that you get involved with. A lot of times I find record labels, in my opinion, are signing artists way before they're ready. Then the artist is getting pissed because radio didn't play them, or this or that, or blah blah blah.

It's not the radio stations' fault that you didn't do your homework. It's not the radio stations' fault that your artist can't perform. It's not the radio stations' fault that most of the artists you bring them don't know how to communicate with people, or make eye contact, or have firm handshakes, or decide that if they're chicks they want to have crapped up fingernails and look like a slob. That is not the radio stations' fault.

On the other hand, the artists, in my opinion, need to earn the right to get a release. Too often I think we're falling in love with the song or we're falling in love with the music. Or we see this person do one song and we get really excited. We put the ball in motion and off we are to the races.

The problem with that is once you get them out on radio tour, and once the studio time has been done, and once the setup's been done, you're a couple of hundred-thousand dollars in. You may find out that artist is a total jerk off. Or that artist can't wake up at 6:00 in the morning. Or that artist manufactured that sound in the studio. We had that problem happen one time.

It's like me throwing one great pass and thinking that I should be the quarterback of the Denver Broncos. It's not going to happen. There's a lot more to it than just throwing one perfect pass. I better understand the blitz or I'm going to get killed.

I'm overweight. I'm 46 years old. The odds of me having a career in the NFL are not there no matter how good of a pass, no matter how good of 100 passes in a row, I throw. Once I get in the game it's completely different. That's the same thing with the record business. It's more than just singing. It's more than just performing.

It all starts with the song. Let me throw that out there. I'm not saying that the music can absolutely suck. But it is not the end all be all. There are other things that we need to think about.

I was talking with Scott Borchetta of Big Machine Label Group. I consider him a historian. He's been around for a long time. I said Scott I've been racking my brain. I am trying to figure out if I can recall an artist who got dropped from their label for selling way too many records or having way too many fans. Of course we both laughed because that's not the case.

If that's the one thing that can determine whether a record company makes money or an artist gets to keep their career, why wouldn't that be the sole focus before the major investment and before taking that song to radio? If the one thing that controls everything is sales, or fans, why is less time spent on fan development and teaching the artist how to engage their fan base before we throw, you know, half a million dollars to go work a single to radio and try to build it that way?

It's beyond me. Everyone thinks Taylor Swift came out of nowhere. Taylor Swift was building her fans and working on her craft for four years before she ever stepped foot in a radio station.

Everyone says, "Oh, if you sell 100,000 downloads you should forget the record deal." Ask Florida Georgia Line how that would've worked out for them. They DID go out and sell 100-thousand downloads on their own. They DID develop as writers. They DID continue to go play college parties and small bars while working on their live show.

Do you want to guess what happened after they signed their deal with Big Machine Label Group? They signed on a Monday, shipped their single to radio Monday night, charted on a Tuesday, 15 weeks later had their first #1, and I think right now they're up to six-point-two MILLION downloads of one particular song that they had sold 100,000 on their own. Would that have happened without the record label? Absolutely not. There's no way that they would've been able to get that kind of traction in that short a period of time to become the superstars they are today.

What did Florida Georgia Line and Taylor Swift have that most people don't have? They had work ethic and they wanted to show that they were different. When Taylor came along, Taylor didn't sound like anyone else. She sounded like Taylor Swift and that's what scared people.

When Florida Georgia Line came along, they showcased for every label. Every label knew who they were. Heck, their manager and the publishing company, Craig Wiseman, Big Loud Shirt, had written hundreds of hit songs. But Florida Georgia Line sounded like Florida Georgia Line. They didn't sound like anyone, either. That scared people.

So, what Taylor did is she went to MySpace and she created her own audience. Florida Georgia Line invested in themselves, put a good team together, and they went out and showed there was a market for what they do. So the perception changed. The music didn't change. The lyrics didn't change. The melody didn't change. The perception changed. Today you cannot turn on a radio station without hearing Taylor Swift or Florida Georgia Line over and over and over again.

So, here's the deal: Do you need a major label record deal to have a career in the music business? Absolutely not. Do you need a record label if you want to have world domination in the music industry? In my opinion, I believe so.

What's the best way to get it? Go out there and prove that there are people that are hungry for you and your music. Too often we create the product first and then we try to go force-feed it to an audience. And the labels, I hate to say it, are as guilty as everyone else for doing that.

Right now you have the ability with the Internet... and now I'm speaking to both independent artists and any industry people or label people that might be reading this...you have the ability to get in front of an audience 24-hours a day, seven days a week and find out if there's a hungry audience for what it is that you're trying to feed them before you ever have to make a major investment in anything.

Why would you not take advantage of that? Why would you not spend some time? Who cares if it takes a year or two years? Shit, we're not curing cancer; we're in the music business. If it takes two years, three years, if it even takes four years to build a solid fan base of hungry consumers why wouldn't that be the focus?

Right now I think we need to spend more time in marketing seminars. That's where I've spent the last year and a half, and it's been absolutely a blast to open up and see why it is that our industry, which creates more content than anyone in the world, is not doing as well as it could be online.

Like I said, this is my opinion and my opinion only. A lot of people are going to bitch. A lot of people are going to think 'who the hell does Rick Barker think he is?' I'm just a guy that's got an opinion, but I'm a guy that bases my opinion on facts. You can go fact check anything.

Go find me an artist that's been dropped from a major label or because they had way too many fans. You can go find artists who've had great chart position who no longer have their record deals. So, obviously, radio's not the end all be all and radio is not your savior. Once again, the fans are your saviors, not radio. How can somebody have a number two song and then their next song fail and then be dropped from a record label? Because they didn't sell enough records.

And, artists stop bitching at the labels. They are the banks, and the bank is going to put the best deal possible to get their investment back. I read an article the other day saying labels rip off the artists and that the artists don't make any money. Well, most of the time, neither do the labels on that particular artist. There are more failures every year than there are successes. It's just the successes pay really well. So, I would be doing everything in my power to go out there and be a success.

Why Bands Need to Stop Bitching About Venues

Wade Sutton, Rocket to the Stars

I am writing this article fully aware of how likely it is that the comment section below will turn into a blood bath. This is a very touchy subject with a lot of singers and bands and I'm certain some as hostile and overly critical will see my brutal honesty. But those that know me well are well aware that I am extremely supportive of artists and want to see them succeed.

Readers should also keep in mind that I have personal experience when it comes to nearly every angle of the issue at hand. I've been a part of shows in which the venues did nothing to promote what we had going on. I've headed up promotions for shows, including Rocket's own artist development competition. I have asked questions of owners and operators of venues as well as professional promoters. And during nearly two decades working as a radio journalist, I have witnessed how various types of legislation and the economy have harmed the very restaurants and bars many of you want to play.

Got all that? This is really long but, if you stick with me, you might learn something.

Saxophonist Dave Goldberg got a lot of attention for an open letter he wrote a while back to operators of venues that host live music. The letter was Goldberg's way of sounding off against venues not paying artists as much money as they feel they deserve. The text, while not hostile in nature, was extremely misguided and managed to ignite another round of firestorms by similarly misguided artists. It was missing a lot of important information concerning why the music scene is the way it is right now and really offered little in the way of how to improve it other than to say venues should simply pay bands more money. Making matters worse, and this should have been expected, the comment section under the article turned into yet another "people need to support live music" scream session.

So I spent the past five or six days thinking about what Goldberg wrote and took into consideration the points he was trying to make...and I came to the conclusion that I could not disagree with him more. See, it is easy for singers and musicians to criticize venues for not paying them more money to perform. It is easy to use the anonymity of the Internet to lash out at the venues just like it is easy to complain about it when in the company of other musicians who feel the same way. But many artists find it easier to be critical in this situation than it is to sit down and take a hard look at WHY things are the way they are... because to do so properly involves a massive amount of self-evaluation. That is something most artists simply refuse to do even though it could be the key to a more successful music career.

Where to begin?

The fine line between "art" and "business"...

You can be an "artist" in the privacy of your own home or when you are recording or when you are playing at an event that doesn't involve money. But once you step into the realm of playing in exchange for cash, you leave the sanctuary of being an "artist" and enter the no-holds-barred world of "business." That changes the rules quite drastically because the level of expectations becomes much different and you suddenly introduce several variables over which you have little or no control. Once money is involved you become a businessman (or woman), a marketer, and a customer service representative.

The music business is a business of relationships and you need to have good relationships with your fans as well as the venues at which you are hoping to play. Yet I see so many of you burning bridges by publicly blasting the venue operators for not giving you what you want instead of creating a better situation for yourselves. And you CAN make a better situation for yourselves. I know you can because there are bands out there right now "making it" just fine, only they aren't sitting around bitching and moaning about the current state of things and are instead finding new ways to thrive in the evolving business environment.

When venues won't promote your show...

In a perfect world, venues would be just as enthusiastic about promoting your shows in their house as you are. Sadly, it isn't a perfect world. I had the honor of being involved in a truly wonderful show at the Hard Rock Cafe in Pittsburgh. I was the show's writer and host and, taking my role in shows as seriously as I do, I was present for every rehearsal for the months leading up to it (yes, we rehearsed for MONTHS for one show...and lived to tell about it).

A few weeks before the show was scheduled to take place, one of the performers brought to our attention that Hard Rock not only wasn't trying to promote the show, the venue hadn't even put it on their website's schedule. The show's producer, James Meny, attempted to contact Hard Rock about the issue to no avail. Relatives of some of the performers in the show started calling the restaurant wanting to know why it wasn't on the site's schedule. Nobody could get any answers. Were we upset about it? Of course we were. How did the performers in the show respond? They kicked their ticket selling efforts into high gear and, not only did they sell out the venue, the Hard Rock that night was over capacity.

You wish venues would do more to promote your shows. I understand that. But this is an issue you have little or no control over. So you can refuse to play those venues or you can accept it for what it is and find ways to improve your own marketing skills (something you should be doing anyway). I can tell you this though: Whining and complaining will change nothing other than a venue's desire to have you back.

Paying your band is a risk for the venue, not an asset...

Put on your "business goggles" and look at your band through the eyes of a venue operator and you will see a financial risk, not an asset. This happens for a lot of reasons. Many of you fail to stop and think about how many other bands walk into a venue on a daily basis and shower the owners with promises of sold out shows. Then the night of the show arrives and you bring in around 100 people. Why is this such a huge financial risk for the venue? Not only would they be in the hole for what they agreed to pay you for performing, the owners would have scheduled too many employees to work (waitresses, bartenders, cooks, hostesses, dish-washers, bussers, etc.). That is a lot of money to not make back because you made empty promises about crowds you knew you couldn't bring. And imagine how pissed off the employees would be if they were told they had to work on a Friday or Saturday night only to get sent home two hours into the shift. In that case, not only is the venue out a lot of money, now their employees are unhappy.

Want to know how you can clear this hurdle? Develop a strong reputation for drawing big crowds on a consistent basis. There are two things you can do to start down that road.

The first tip is to start putting a serious and legitimate effort into collecting e-mails and expanding your fan base. And don't just collect e-mails, segment them. That means be sure to get the zip codes of every person signing up. Want to impress a venue owner and put yourself in a better BUSINESS position to leverage more money? Slap down a list of 800 e-mail subscribers all living within a twenty mile drive of the venue. That is 800 people you can market to directly about that show.

The second tip goes hand-in-hand with the first. Many of you need to start branching out and stop playing in the same geographical area night after night. I see so many bands doing two and three shows a week, every week, in an area of about a 20-mile radius. I'm not talking about bands in major cities; I'm seeing this from bands in rural areas. You are damaging the demand for your product, which is weakening your business leverage against the venue.

People are less likely to come to your show on a Friday night when they know they can see you Saturday or Sunday night... or sometime next week. So many of you are burning out your audiences and it is ruining your ability to get more money from venue operators. Stop saying, "I'll start playing venues that are farther away when I have more fans coming to my shows here". Go do it NOW so you can build up your fan base, play more cities, and make your shows back home MEAN something when they happen.

You are worth what somebody is willing to pay you...

I'm so tired of hearing bands saying, "I understand the economy sucks right now but I deserve to be paid more." First of all, you deserve to be paid what the market dictates you should be paid. If the highest payment you can find for your act is one hundred dollars per show, well, I hate to break it to you but you are a one hundred dollar band. Stop bitching about it and start looking for ways to improve your worth (like building up your e-mail lists and creating a better live show). When you are WORTH two thousand dollars per show, you will make two thousand dollars per show.

And as far as the economy is concerned, restaurants and bars have been hurt by far more than just the economy, something you would know if some of you would take some time to sit down and TALK to these venue owners instead of bitching about them from behind a computer screen. They have a laundry list of reasons for being so mindful of the money going out right now.

First off, many restaurants and bars are still trying to recover from when public smoking bans were enacted in several states. The drop in business was experienced almost immediately. That came around the same time as the passage of bills promoting ethanol-based fuels, which resulted in massive spikes in food prices that were either absorbed by the restaurants and bars or passed down to customers. More recently, the Affordable Care Act struck and insurance premiums skyrocketed for both employers and employees. If all that wasn't enough to make them tighten the purse strings, keep in mind that whenever states have a pet project they want to fund, taxes on alcohol and tobacco are often the first targets. What do you think happens to restaurants and bars when the price of alcohol goes up? It isn't good, I can tell you that. And now restaurants are staring down the possibility of steep increases in dairy prices. Ever consider how many items on menus are smothered in cheese? Oh, and don't forget that many of these establishments are already paying thousands of dollars a year to organizations like ASCAP, SESCA, and BMI for music licensing.

So when you approach a venue and get so bent out of shape because they won't pay you more money, don't assume that their financial books are as rosy as many others think. Get off your butts and do something to make them want to move you from the "risk" column to the "calculated risk" column.

Want people to support live music?
GIVE THEM A REASON TO...

Going back to the constant cries about people not supporting local music. Let's be honest with each other: Many of you (not all) have live shows that suck. Before you get all bent out of shape about me saying that, take this into consideration: Are you aware of how many of you put on live shows that are nothing more than background music? I'm talking about audiences that are not watching you because they are talking to each other, eating or drinking, looking at their phones, and leaving early. If that is what is happening at your show, then the venues are seeing you as nothing better than a jukebox (which they probably already spent money on). That is part of the reason why they don't want to pay many of you more money.

I will give you two reasons why people are not "supporting local music" and you can do what you want with the information. The first reason is because people don't want to shell out money for a cover charge, pay to park, fork over cash for food and drinks, make a quick stop at the gas station, not to mention pay a babysitter just to see a band that isn't all that entertaining in person. Just because YOU are having fun on stage doesn't mean the audience is having fun. The second big reason is because you are failing in your mission to compete against every other form of entertainment available to your fans. The amount of money people have to spend on entertainment is like a pie and there are only so many pieces to go around. Remember earlier when I said you are a business? Businesses COMPETE whether you like it or not.

When two people have a certain amount of money each month to spend on entertainment, they are trying to decide between your show, shows by every other band, movies, sporting events, clubs with DJs, live theater, going skiing, shopping at the mall, buying a new television, amusement parks, video games, banking that money for vacation, and every other form of entertainment available. And YOU want these people to pass up their other options and spend their hard earned money on YOU when you won't even spend the time to put together a top-notch live show? If you want them to come out and "support live music," you are going to have to become the better option.

I know some of this sounds extremely harsh but the reality of the situation is I REALLY want to see more artists finding success with their music. And many of the artists having successful careers in music have managed to move past all the garbage talked about in this article. They understand that music is more about business than even the music itself... and they have done what all good business people do.

They don't waste time complaining and find ways to adapt.

CHAPTER 4

The Truth Behind Radio

Understanding Radio

Rick Barker, Music Industry Blueprint's
"25 Minutes From Nashville"

A lot of independent artists want to know when it is the right time for them to take their song to radio. And I think before I can answer that, I need to explain to those that don't know, and some that think they might know, what it is that radio actually does. Every business has its own set of goals and they may not necessarily align with your goals. What you want to do is find the best way to help them achieve their goal and, if you can incorporate yourself into that, you've hit a homerun.

So think about it: What is the goal of a radio station? The goal of a radio station is to sell advertising. That is the only way radio stations generate revenue. It's not from playing music. It's not from having a sports talk station. They make their revenue from a commercial and that's called traditional revenue. You'll hear some people say, "Radio stations are really looking for ways to create NTR." That means nontraditional revenue, things other than

48

commercials. And that's where I found some pretty good success in being able to get radio stations to support new artists.

So the goal of the radio station is to make money. The way that they make money is by selling advertising. The way that they get to charge more for their advertising is by having higher ratings. How do you get higher ratings? You have people listen longer. How do you get people to listen longer? You give them what they want. What they want, it seems, is music that they're familiar with and music they already know.

When you're driving down the road and you hear the same song pop up every couple hours, it is because they have something in larger markets now called the people meter and PPM market. A PPM market and the people meter can tell you exactly when people are tuning in or tuning out. It's just like analytics you can get on your videos to know when people are watching or turning it off. So the people meter can tell you what songs they are staying for, what songs they leaving because of, and how far into a commercial break are they actually listening. That's where radio's going to start getting screwed because the traditional form of advertising is commercials and how many of you listen to commercials. I know I don't. I know that right now I fast-forward all the commercials. We have become an instant society.

So now radio stations are scrambling to figure out how they can create non-traditional revenue to make up for the folks that didn't hear the commercials that people were charged for. So this is where you could come into play. You need to show them, as an artist, manager, or record label, that there's demand in that particular market for you or your artist.

Too many people are trying to go out and get world domination first and get national exposure. I think that's wrong. I think that you need to start in your hometown. And let me say this, and I say this out of respect: If you can't be the best thing in your town, you're not going to be the best thing in the world. You may end up there one day but immediately, if you can't show me or a program director or a record company or an advertiser that you are relevant in your own market, then that's going to put you way back as far as everyone else is concerned.

So what you want to do is show that you're relevant in your market and that is why I'm advocating segmenting email lists. Because, as you're using the Internet to get all this exposure, by segmenting e-mails you can go on to your email database and say, "Okay, let me see everyone who's within 50 miles of Nashville." And let's say your email database comes back that you have 200 people that are within 50-miles of Nashville. Then you take that data and you start marketing and engaging with those folks.

The first step in marketing, for me, is to make sure that they have your music. And it's not by selling your music. You can't. The first time someone gets to hear your music or have your music they shouldn't have to pay for it. There are too many options for them.

So you market to them by inviting them to have your music and get to know your music. Then every other week you're continuing to build this relationship through engaging emails and conversation and interaction on your social media sites. And then what you're able to do is reach out to them and say, "Okay, I want to come do a show in your area. Where is it that you think that I should play?" They're going to tell you the clubs that you need to contact. Then you're going to be able to reach out to the club.

Now, you have probably noticed we haven't gone to radio yet. This is the buildup. So you are going to go to that club and say, "I'm going to be traveling through town and I have quite a few fans in your area. They're the ones that told me to contact you. I would love to either open for someone or have a night that I can perform." And they're going to hopefully ask you questions like how many people. When you respond that you have emails from people in the area they will be like, "Oh, you have 200 people that you've built a relationship with that know your music?" Now, if you've done the relationship part right, those people can't wait to meet you because you're not in their town all the time. So you go ahead and book yourself a show, you go ahead and sell your own tickets online, you go ahead and create your own bundles that have merchandise packages and all kinds of cool stuff that these fans are going to show off.

Another trick you could do is you could go to the bar owner and say, "How much do you charge your employees for beers and would you be willing to sell me employee pricing on your beers?" In most places it's like a buck. So what you do is you spend a hundred dollars and you buy a hundred drink tickets and then you go and say, "Hey, for the first hundred people that come to the show I'm going to buy your first beer. Come have a beer with me." Costs you a hundred dollars but if you just sold your tickets for 10 dollars you just made 900. Don't be afraid to invest money to make money.

Then you're able to go to the local radio station and say, I'm coming to town and I'm doing a sold-out show. Find a venue that is small that you can sell out. The word sell out is awesome. Say, "I'm coming to town to do a sold-out show and I would love to give you guys the opportunity to hang a banner if you'd like." Or, "I would love to give you the opportunity." This is what Billboard magazine features the story on, that opportunity I created. Say, "Hey, how would you like to give my music away through your Facebook and Twitter page and maybe some tickets to the sold-out show? Now you're relevant. Now they've got something that no one else can get with your tickets to the sold-out show. Now you're not asking them for airplay. You're not asking them to do anything that's going to jeopardize the fact that they have to play this familiar music in order to sell commercials.

Most of the time the bars are clients of the radio station, so the bars will include you in the advertising. Many times, bars can be the worst clients for radio stations because they can be the worst at paying their bills. So you may want to make sure, by going and doing a little research on the radio stations' websites or Facebook pages, if they do advance with these bars. Try to target bars or venues that the radio station already has a relationship with and enhance that relationship.

A better thing that you can do to build awareness in a market is to contact the people who spent the most money at radio stations. They are usually car dealerships and local markets. Contact the local car dealer and let him know, "I'm in a band and we're actually coming to play in a few weeks at a club in your area. I was wondering, how many people during the week would you say test-drive your cars?" Ask to speak to a sales guy and they're going to tell you. Then you say, "I was wondering if I could send a box of CDs and would you mind giving them away with everyone who test-drives a car? By the way, I'm coming to town to do a sold-out show and I would love to give you a couple tickets for you to come in and see the show."

So now if this car dealer all of a sudden says that they do a hundred test-drives in a week then you go and produce a hundred CDs. They're not expensive to duplicate now. Send them to that dealership and now you have 200 or 100 more people who will know your music and who will be familiar with it in that market. And then at the show you build the relationship with those fans and you give them opportunities to follow you on your social media. And you start thanking the radio station for their support. It doesn't matter that they didn't play you. If they answer the phone, they supported you. Thank them for their support. Start including them in your hashtags and they'll start re-tweeting because the people who control the social media sites of the radio stations are not necessarily the program director or music director... they're the promotion people. And promotion people have Google alerts so every time something is said about their radio station, they re-tweet it.

Now your tweets are being re-tweeted in that radio market. Then you're going to encourage people, "Hey, guys, go follow the local radio station." Don't ask them to play your music yet. Just say, "Hey, go follow the local radio station. I really want to show them I appreciate what they did to support me."

Here is where the strategy comes into play: After the show, if you've done everything right and you segmented, they've signed up for your access list where you're going to be able to communicate with them, send the follow-up with either pictures from the meet and greet or if you created a photo album on your Facebook page with pictures from the meet and greet. And make sure they have a link that says, "Here is what I would love for you to do. I can't wait to come back and see you. I need you to start reaching out and commenting on the radio stations' Facebook pages and on the radio station's Twitters, about what a great time you had at my show. And then when the time is right I'm going to ask you guys to start contacting them and requesting my song."

The problem that most people have is they try to do everything in one day. They try to get on the radio, they try to get the venue, they try to get the fans, and they try to do everything in one day. It is a process. And there is a tactical strategy involved with this process. Most people just can't book a show, and announce on their website or Twitter feed, "Hey, I'm coming to town to do a show." There is no real thought that goes into what you can do to make the show the best show possible. Most don't even plan their set list before they get there. That is the biggest disservice that you can do to a fan who has paid money to come see you, to be that unorganized. And that's what I love about Tom Jackson and what he teaches with his program.

I hope you understand radio a little bit better. Oh! One more thing about the car lots. The car dealers could actually include you in their advertising. So if you have gone and done the work to create a sold-out show, they could include that in their advertising. Bring this up to them. You say, "Listen, I would love to give you a couple of pair of tickets to the sold-out show and meet-and-greet access. People can stop by your car lot and register to win."

So, when they run their ads that week, they could say, "Stop by and test drive the new Chevrolet and while you're here, everyone who test drives this weekend receives a free CD from Rick Barker. He's got a sold out show coming up and we will give you a chance to register to win tickets and meet and greet and backstage passes. So head on over to blah blah blah!" Now you got advertisement on the radio station that you don't have to pay for. Now your name is being spread out there.

And when you call the radio station and invite them to be a part of your sold-out show, the thing that is going to go through their mind is, "How did this person sell out a show in our market with no radio play and no support from the radio station?" They're going to see that you did that because you have access to their consumers. You have access to their listeners. And now you're starting to make yourself relevant in that particular market for that particular radio station. Not EVERY radio station in the country, but THAT particular station in THAT particular market.

You're able to start building your relationships in your regions one step at a time. The key is to become kick butt in your area and then step out a hundred miles. And then step out a hundred miles more and then take everything you've done within those hundred miles and, over the next couple of years, have data that you can actually present and say, "This is where I'm relevant, this is why I'm relevant, and this is how much I have sold. This is the communication I have with my fan base. This is the support that I have on my social networks." Now you've become a partner for a radio station.

What Happens on Radio Tour (Part 1)

Rick Backer, Music Industry Blueprint's ### *"25 Minutes From Nashville"*

I know everyone gets excited about having their song played on the radio. That's why a lot of people get in this. Ask them, "What's your goal?" and they say, "Oh I just can't wait to have my song heard on the radio." You need to understand the pros and cons. Well, the pros are great. You get on the radio and your song blows up.

I am going to talk about country music because I am here in Nashville and I see this happening all the time. Millions upon millions upon millions of dollars have gone down the drain and, had people known the information that I am about to give you, it would have saved a lot of people a lot of money, a lot of time, and a lot of heartache.

So, here is the deal. Days have changed. Where radio stations used to be in the old days, as you hear people talking about, you could just take a song in to a DJ, the DJ would get excited about it, and they'd play the music. You would hear that story all the time back when Elvis and Mo-Town and a lot of the early rock bands were around back in the 50s, 60s, 70s, and possibly even some of the 80s.

Well, that all started changing in the 90s. In the 90s, Bill Clinton passed an act, which allowed radio stations to own more than one station in multiple markets and that's when the Clear Channels became big, and Cumulus and CBS, and things like that. So that was around 1996, around the time the Internet started. When that happened, you had major corporations controlling a lot of stations and they would start putting in place these "Regional Program Directors" so the music decisions, a lot of times, weren't even being made inside the building. So that gets you caught up as far as the transition on how things happen.

Let's bring it to today. It's harder to get on the radio today because there are less quality spots available in hours where people actually hear the music. There's still just 24 hours in a day but songs need to go through their progressions. And their progressions usually start with a light rotation, which is in the middle of the night. Medium rotation might start getting a play sometime between 7:00 pm and midnight, then a heavy rotation when it just gets nailed all the time.

You know, you're hearing the song all the time. Well, if you notice, there are only about twenty of those songs. So, if the major record labels are out there competing for the same twenty spots and you are an independent artist trying to compete for the same twenty spots, and they have relationships and a proven track record, how hard do you think it's going to be for YOU to break through? It's going to be very hard. That's why it doesn't happen.

That's why we haven't had an independent artist without a major record label behind them, and I will recheck the numbers, but I don't think they have been able to crack the Top 20. I think they might have gotten close but they haven't been able to crack the Top 20 and the deal is you don't really start making money on your single until it gets into the Top 20. That's if you happen to own the single because the only people making money on the first radio single are the publishers and the writer of the song. It's not the record company and it's not the artist. Radio airplay pays whom? It pays publishers and writers!

Then Spotify came along and they now pay the record label, but that's a whole other thing for me to talk about. So, right now, if you didn't write the song and if you convinced somebody to let you take the song to radio, you are not making money as the writer and you are not making money as the publisher, but you are the one spending all the money to get seen.

Here is how much it costs to take a song to radio. First, you're going to go and have to record the song. That's going cost you anywhere between five- to ten-thousand dollars to get the song radio-ready. There are a couple of guys that mix the songs. They understand the compression and the way that radio likes these songs to sound, so figure probably right around ten thousand dollars. Then you're going to have to pay a promotion staff to work that song to radio. That promotion staff, if you are going after major market radio, is going to cost you on the low end ten-thousand dollars a month, on the high end 15-thousand dollars a month. Plus, you are going to have to pick up all your expenses for driving in to these radio stations. You're going to have to pick up the expenses on the marketing.

So go ahead and figure between 20- and 25-thousand dollars a month for this to happen. Right now it takes a brand new artist, if they are lucky, being out at radio stations for six months leading up to before they ever release their single. Okay? So that's six months times 20-thousand dollars, that's 120-thousand dollars.

Now you go for your add day. Now you are going to have to continue to keep the radio team working. Right now it's taking even established artists 40 to 50 weeks. So let's take another ten months and times that by 20-thousand. That's another 200-thousand dollars. So now you are into this thing for 300-thousand dollars.

They are going to say you probably need a video to make things happen. You are going to go spend 50-thousand dollars on a video. Now you are in 350-thousand dollars on a system that hasn't worked up to this point, in a situation where you are not even getting into a position yet where you can start reaping the benefits of having a charted single IF you happen to get one. Right now, if you go to media base there's 178 songs all trying to get into that Top 20 and, most of the time, your songs aren't as good as the songs in the Top 20. They're just not.

You are not expected to be there yet, but everyone thinks just cause they can record a record and they can afford to go on radio tour that they should be there and it gets real, real expensive and then, what happens, is your radio team comes back and starts telling you things like, "Wow you know, we weren't expecting Taylor Swift to release a record and, you know, it's really hard right now cause, you know, you don't have this and you don't have that". And they are just talking heads at that point but they did what you asked them to do. They took your song to the radio. Yes, they can go take a song to radio. Can they get it played? No guarantees. There are no guarantees that they can even get it heard and that's the sad part right now. The hardest part is getting your song heard.

So that's not meant to scare you. It's just to let you know it is very expensive to take a song to radio no matter how much money you have. If they could be bought, we would have more Taylors. I always say that. The radio station's role is to sell advertising to make money. The program director and the music director, their job every day, is not to lose their job.

So you go out and show them that there's a reason. That's why I promote breaking regionally. It's less expensive and it's easier to build relationships. You are from North Carolina? You don't try to convince California radio stations to play you. There is no reason for them to play you. Now, if you end up on a major label because you have gone out and built a following regionally and got some regional air play and you have ticket sales to show in that region, you are going to be much more attractive to a label. And that goes back to what I have said in the past: go make yourself a partner."

Avoiding Radio Interview Pitfalls

Wade Sutton, Rocket to the Stars

I heard the most atrocious radio interview one Thursday afternoon while driving. The interview was between a reporter and a football player for the University of Pittsburgh. It was prerecorded and was airing as part of the pregame coverage leading into the Little Caesar's Pizza Bowl in Detroit where Pitt was taking on Bowling Green. I was only a minute or two into the interview before

I unleashed a string of obscenities at the radio and changed it to something that was easier to listen to.

What was so bad about the interview? Well, let's start with the fact that the player being interviewed was rambling and talking so quickly that it left him literally gasping for air every time he inhaled. And I know what you are probably thinking. Come on, Wade. The guy is a college football player and isn't used to doing interviews. That is the thing: It wasn't just the Pitt football player who sounded like he was trying to suck down the microphone with every breath. The reporter was doing it too! And they were both mouth-breathing the entire time. I still wonder if that poor microphone survived the interview.

Radio interviews are tools for you to promote your act, website, and show...

I know this is going to sound harsh but you need to keep your head on straight and remember that doing a radio interview is part of your music business. It needs to be taken very seriously because a lot of people (hopefully) are listening. I have seen and heard a lot of singers and bands walk into a radio studio and it's like they just walked on stage at the Opry. They end up losing focus during the interview and it sounds awful. Do not allow yourself to get "caught up in the moment." I know for people not accustomed to being in a radio studio, actually being there can feel glamorous and make you feel like you are "on your way." I'm here to tell you to cut that crap out right now. Just... stop it! When you are rich and famous and your audience is married to you, then you can sit back during the interview and soak it all in. But at this point most of you are trying to sell tickets to that night's show so you can put gas in your Scion.

Have a mental list of things you can talk about and stories you can tell...

Short story to illustrate a perfectly good point: One of my earliest radio interviews was with former U.S. Congressman Ron Klink (D-Pa). I spotted him at a community event and ran over to ask him a question about some hot-button issue that had been in the news at the time. We probably needed a bridge fixed or something. Bridges in Pennsylvania are widely considered the worst in the country. Anyway... I got his answer on tape, went back to the radio station to cut the audio, and aired the sound bytes during my newscasts the following morning.

Then something funny happened. Later that day I was watching the news on one of the Pittsburgh television stations and there is Congressman Klink at a different event, being asked about the same issue I had grilled him about the previous day. You know what happened? He gave the exact same answer he gave me one day before. Exact...same...answer. Word...for...word. I remember thinking to myself, "WTF?" Only I was thinking the entire phrase because Internet acronyms didn't really exist yet.

You need to think ahead of time about how you are going to respond to certain questions. You also need to take some of your funniest, saddest, most entertaining stories and PRACTICE telling them. Work on your delivery. Keep those answers and stories in your back pocket because you will need them at some point during an interview. Your fans are fans because they want you to entertain them. Part of that entertainment comes through the stories you tell and how you go about communicating them.

Leave NOTHING to chance...

I have seen so many singers, bands, politicians, professional athletes, community figureheads and others fall victim to bad interviews because the person interviewing them was bad at their job. Interviews are a lot like dancing in that both people need to know what they are doing for it to come off really well. If one of you sucks at it, it will be extremely awkward for those watching/listening and you will be made fun of. In blogs like this one.

There are two things you should always do prior to a live radio interview. The first thing you need to do is get on the phone and call the person interviewing you. Talk to them. Strike up a conversation and get a feel for what to expect when you are actually on the radio during the interview. The second thing you should do is send the interviewer some talking points so they know some of the things you want to be sure to cover during the radio segment. It is preemptively taking control of YOUR interview before you even step foot in the studio. Word to the wise: Send bullet points instead of written questions. If you write out questions and send them to a bad interviewer, they will simply sit there and read the questions from the paper. Like a robot. And it will make people change the station before the interview is done.

Warm up your voice prior to the interview...

I am going to toss out an idea that will make some of you think I've completely lost my mind. You might want to sit down for it. Ready? Here it comes: If you are doing a radio interview during morning drive, specifically the much-coveted seven o'clock hour, you need to roll yourselves out of bed by four. I will wait for you to stop laughing. Done? Good.

You are a singer. You are going on the radio to talk about the fact that you sing. You know what they might ask you to do during the interview? They might ask you to sing. Some of us wake up in the morning sounding like a cross between Darth Vader and my chain-smoking grandmother. Many people need to be up for a few hours before our voices sound the best they can sound. If you are on the air at seven, get up at four so you have time to warm up your voice prior to going on the air. Stand outside the studio and sing before the interview. The radio staffs dig that kind of thing. It's like watching a professional athlete warm up before the game. People actually take pictures of that sort of thing.

Learn the art of changing the subject...

At some point in your career you are going to cross paths with a radio DJ who either got up on the wrong side of the bed that morning, is having an all-around bad day, or suddenly decides he has something to prove. You will sit down for your interview stoked to be talking about that night's show at the Hard Rock and all of a sudden you are being asked about your feelings on the failed Middle East peace accord or something else that you know absolutely nothing about. So what do you do? You learn to take control of the interview and keep the conversation on what it is supposed to be on: YOU.

The art of changing the subject is a difficult skill to hone. Radio talk show hosts are great at it. Politicians are amazing at it. But it takes a lot of time and practice. And it doesn't just get you out of questions about heavy subjects like religion and politics. It will also help if somebody asks you a question you consider inappropriate or humiliating. Trust me. It happens more than you probably want to believe.

What Happens on Radio Tour (Part 2)

Rick Barker, Music Industry Blueprint's "25 Minutes From Nashville"

I created something that a lot of you might not be aware of called Nashville to You Radio Tour. I was able to take acts that were at the bottom of the chart, that no one had really started playing yet or even heard of, and I created this run in California. That is what actually put me on Big Machine's radar and, really, all the record companies' radars. Because I am the guy who will go out and figure out what the problems are and then come up with some sort of solution. It may not be the right solution, but I at least try. I am not one of those guys that sit around and bitch about all the problems and then do nothing about it. That's just not how I roll.

I had a question about radio tours. Here is what's going to happen: you are going to be brought into these radio stations. You may or may not ever get your song played on the radio. Sometimes you will show up at these radio stations and they may forget you had an appointment with them and you may have driven 500 miles. You may have spent three thousand dollars to get there. That's been known to happen. You may or may not get to perform in the conference room. You may or may not get anything. It may just be a courtesy visit.

So, I am sitting in there going, "Okay, so they are hauling up through these radio stations. They are kind of coming through on their visits they aren't ever putting them in front of an audience." I asked why and I got a couple of different answers. Couple answers were, "no one will show up" and "they are not prepared to be able to play for an hour and they have only got a couple of songs" and I'm wondering "why the hell would you sign somebody who's got only a couple of songs?" I said to them, "Well, here is the deal. You guys are ultimately trying to impress me and I may play it but I am not the one who buys it. Ultimately wouldn't you want to see if your artist could deliver in front of a fan base?" and they were like, "Oh, what a concept!"

So I called a bunch of my radio buddies and I said, "Listen, if I can get us an act, they'll be at the bottom of the charts and they will be new artists, but can we create some kind of new program where we can bring these artists on a consistent basis?" I said, I need to be able to get $1,500 bucks, three hotel rooms and dinner." Now, at the time, record companies were giving these shows away. They were like, "there is no way you will get radio to pay blah, blah, blah, blah, blah, because we have to pay radio," and I said, "The problem is you guys are talking to the wrong person in the building. If I create a program that the sales manager can go out and sell, then all of a sudden I am being told what act I need to play in order to support that show." So then they went, "Oh, okay."

The deal that I would make with the radio stations would be like, "I am not saying you have got to play the song all the time but I am saying you do have to support the act. If you are not interested in supporting the act, no problem. We will go find somebody else who is." I am big on just laying my cards out up front. A lot of people kind of tip toe around things. I have never been that person and that's why I don't get jammed up a lot is because I kind of know what we have going on and I encourage you to do that. So just kind of lay it out on the line first.

If they said "no," we go to another one. So I lined up all these great radio stations. I had my station in San Andreas right there in Santa Barbara, had Santa Maria, San Louis, San Jose, Sacramento, Fresno, to Larry to Baker Field. You could just kind of go up the 101 and back down the 5 and I got flown out to Nashville. I had this idea and everybody loved it and then all of a sudden I go back home to California and nobody calls and there is nothing. No activity and I'm like, "Wait a minute. You guys loved this idea. I have radio stations waiting to give you money, waiting to give you air play," and that's when I learned that people have tunnel vision. They are in their own world trying to get things done.

What I had to do was even go one step further. I had to figure out how to solve people's problems. That's the big thing. If you could solve a problem, you would become a very popular person. So I called them again and I am like, "Look, the act will make $7,500. The first $1,500 will pay to fly them out there and pay for the player and then they get to keep the rest. No one else." I figured most of the young artists don't ever make money, much less get paid out on radio tour.

So I told them that and the next thing you know I get a call and they say, "Hey, we have this kid and he's got this song. It's doing okay on the secondary radio. Major market radio won't really touch it yet but if it can work in California, it can work anywhere," and I said, "Well, who've you got?" They said, "It's Josh Turner and the song is called Long Black Train." Now, I was already playing this song because I lived in an area, you know, my town loves God. There is no problem in playing songs with God in it.

So Josh Turner was the first act we took out. It was awesome. Then I took out Sugarland, Julie Roberts, Jamie O'Neal, Little Big Town, Rodney Atkins, Pat Green and all the Texas acts started doing really well and then that opened up opportunities for me to go into Big Machine Records. The reason I am saying this to you right now is because I had to run and create relationships in a small area where I could deliver results. And I was able to deliver results with the "Nashville To You" tour because I focused on the state of California.

Then "Nashville To You" toured all these other radio stations and they had me speak on a panel at CRS and all these other radio stations started wanting to get involved with it. And I had one in Wisconsin and then I was trying to get four or five others to do it. It didn't make sense and then people would give up. So I learned the hard way about trying to get too big, too fast, and spread out. So that's why I really like to focus on becoming a regional success story so you can go build relationships. It doesn't have to be with the biggest radio stations in that town. It can be with a few small stations in that town.

Start generating some activity in those smaller markets. Stop by the radio stations and say, "Hey, I'd love to just stop by and say hello." It's much easier to get a meeting with someone when they know you are not asking for anything or just stop by and drop off a package at the front and then tweet the program director or the jockey, whoever is in charge and, in a lot of those smaller markets, the program director also has an on-air shift.

So start making requests on their show, start participating in their show, start letting them see your name over and over again, and make these relationships. And, whenever you are in the area, always at least try to stop by and say hello without being there to ask for anything. They will really appreciate that and that's what happened for me.

I got that reputation, as a program director, of being a guy that would support local musicians and the reason that I did that is because I knew Carrie Underwood and Rascal Flatts and Tim McGraw would not likely come into my radio station. But I figured, man if I get an "in" early with an artist, they might come by and start supporting my radio station and that's what happened. My little radio station started getting treated like a major market radio station and I was being invited to all the parties and I was being a guy to talk to by all when I walked around Country Radio Seminar. A lot of them, very important people at these record companies knew who I was because I was out there making a difference for their younger acts. It is real easy to get behind the superstars. It's really hard to get behind a young act.

So, as a young act, what do you need to do in order to get a radio station to look at you? First, have radio-ready material. Most of your songs would not sound good on the radio no matter how great you think they are, or your mom thinks they are, they can't compete. So hone your craft. Make sure your recordings are quality. Like I said, you are going to have to spend some money but you want to take a bunch of demos that you have recorded for $250 or $300 and sit down with someone that you trust and see which song might have the best chance. Then, if it needs to be re-written, re-write it. It definitely will need to be re-recorded for radio. Toss them out to your audience. See which ones are resonating with them but don't go in the studio and spend a whole bunch of freaking money and then expect me to like it.

Most young artists are not re-writing their songs. There are very few songs in Nashville by hit songwriters that don't get re-written at least a couple of times. They take it. They live with it for a little while. They feel what happens. But you want to be taken seriously by radio because you are competing and you are asking them to play you and not play somebody from a label.

You want to make sure your website looks smoking. That it's awesome, that you are active on social media, that you are engaged, that the only way they can tell that you are not already signed to a major label was because you told them. Not because your packaging looks shoddy, not because your quality of your recording sounded like crap, not because of the fact that your website looks like your uncle did it for you for free. You want to present yourself like a rock star and you want to be taken seriously. You have to present yourself seriously. Also, make sure you have at least 45 minutes of material that you can play because, when you walk in and they take you, they may have you play it over and over and over again.

So don't get excited about one song and think you are ready for radio tour because...you are not. Until you are ready, don't put yourself in a position for them to just check you off the list because they are NOT looking for reasons to say "yes" right now. They are looking for reasons to say "no" because it is very crowded. Don't give them any reasons."

CHAPTER 5

The Tools For The Media

Why Electronic Press Kits Are So Important

Wade Sutton, Rocket to the Stars

At the time of this writing, I have had an unusually high number of singers and bands asking questions about whether they really need an electronic press kit if they already have a website. The answer is simple: Yes, you should have both.

I know some people familiar with the services offered by Rocket to the Stars will immediately say something like, "Of course you are going to say bands need both because you create electronic press kits." The truth is actually the complete opposite. Rocket offers the EPK service because it IS such an important part of an artist's music business. Want to know why?

Because the manner in which you communicate with the media is not the same as the manner in which you communicate with your fans. Your fans' needs are much different than the media's needs when it comes to anything involving you, your music, and your music business. So if their needs are so different from each other, the method of communicating with them has to be different.

The TRUE purpose of websites and EPKs...

To understand exactly why the electronic press kit (EPK) is so important from a public and media relations perspective, you have to take a hard look at why both websites and EPKs even exist. The short answer is because websites are visited by fans and EPKs are visited by media and, at times, owners of venues at which you are hoping to do shows.

The entire purpose of your band's website is (or should be) to collect e-mails from fans so that you may communicate with and market to them directly. It is the only presence on the Internet that you have complete control over and is one of the many standards by which people in the music industry judge you on how seriously you are taking your music business. So, again, your website is designed to fill the needs of your fans. Their needs are very basic. Most fans want the following...

1. They want to know what your music sounds like.
2. They want to know how they can obtain your music.
3. They want to know when and where you are playing.
4. Some will want to know a little bit about the band.
5. A way to send you fan e-mails.

That is it. Nothing else. That is why the best band website is only one page, teases fans with a few tracks, and then coaxes them to subscribe to your e-mail list to get downloads of those songs in addition to a few other tracks not available to stream. Any information about the band beyond those basic things should be communicated through the direct e-mails. That is part of the vital "Bribe to Subscribe" back in Chapter 2.

Now let's talk about the purpose of the EPK. If your website is your center of operations for your fans, your EPK is the center of operations for the media, which has entirely different needs. Media people coming to your EPK want to know why you are "newsworthy," which means there is a much greater emphasis on two things: the information contained within the biography (which shows the media member that you are worthy of coverage) and the delivery of everything a member of the media would want or need should they decide to cover you. In other words, you do their job for them and hand them the finished product with a nice bow on top. Nothing will get you further with the media than making them work as little as possible.

So what should your EPK include?

1. Make sure they can stream as much of your music as possible. Do not make somebody visiting your EPK have to download the music to hear it. It isn't a bad idea to offer the tracks for downloading as well (you never know when a radio station program director will visit the EPK and consider playing the music) but the ability to stream the tracks is a must.

2. Pictures. Professionally taken pictures. Not something taken with the camera on your phone. Go to a real photographer and have photographs taken. The EPK should include at least three to five shots and the EPK must allow visitors to be able to download and save all of those pictures. You never know when a reporter writing about you will want to include a photograph. You also never know when the program director at a radio station will want to put your band's picture up on the station's website. Don't make them have to jump through a hoop and ask you for a picture. Be sure those photographs are downloadable via the EPK.

3. Links to all relevant media, including your band's official website, social media, Reverbnation, and music distribution pages (iTunes, Amazon, etc.).

4. A longer, more in-depth biography than what appears on your official website. I will explain more about that in a moment.

5. Any noteworthy testimonials, quotes from and links to professional concert or album reviews, and streams of some past radio interviews (so program directors know you won't sound like a tool on the air).

6. Contact information for the band's manager (phone, e-mail, snail mail). If you don't have a manager, contact information

for the member of the band elected to be your mouthpiece. Don't make the media or program directors have to track you down like a missing child.

The differences in the biographies...

I see a number of artists with official websites and electronic press kits using the same biography on both pages. That is a HUGE mistake.

The biographies on your official website should be short and sweet. The best ones are not longer than three brief paragraphs and jam in as much information as possible. In fact, Rocket did an entire article on writing better biographies. You need to remember that a large number of fans visiting your website will be using mobile devices, many of which are phones. Most people don't read a lot of text on their phone. So, in the case of the bios on your official website, you want to lead with your best foot forward, keep it short and sweet, and make it easy for the reader to retain as much of that information possible.

The biographies on your electronic press kits are a whole different beast. You aren't trying to communicate easy-to-remember facts on this one; you are trying to convince members of the media that you are interesting enough for them to write about you and trying to persuade radio programming directors that their listeners will want to hear and know about you. In other words, why should anybody care about you?

Not only are you trying to show them how and why you are different from every other band, this longer biography also needs to include enough relevant information to allow a print journalist to start writing a story about you. It should include some basic history on not just how the band was formed, but also some background information on each individual member. Some of these biographies can also include short direct quotes from each member. Doing so gives it a more personal feel and journalists love using direct quotes when they write. As I said earlier, it makes their jobs much easier.

So, again, your official website and your electronic press kit are two very different entities. They both exist for the sake of communicating information but they do so in very different ways because they are communicating with different types of people. We always talk about how artists need to "know their audiences". That applies to websites and EPKs just as much as it applies to people listening to your music and attending your shows.

Creating a Better Press Release For Your Band

Wade Sutton, Rocket to the Stars

This development article will undoubtedly upset some public relations people that read it but I am hoping it will serve as a wake-up call for singers and bands either hiring somebody to write press releases about their shows or writing those press releases themselves. I have to start this with a short story that is entirely relevant to the subject matter...

When I was in my early twenties and already a few years into my radio journalism career (I started young), I was kicking around the idea of going back to school to pursue a law degree. I had been covering criminal homicide trials and was fascinated by what goes on in a courtroom. So when I spotted one of our local judges wandering the halls of the county courthouse, I took advantage of the opportunity to ask a few questions.

Wade: I'm thinking about going back to school for law.

Judge: And leave the high paying world of radio? (Snarky laugh)

Wade: Very funny for a guy probably not wearing anything under that robe. What should I major in for undergrad? Political science? Criminal justice? History?

Judge: English.

Wade: Huh? Really? Why that?

Judge: Because being an attorney involves writing an incredible amount of legal briefs and many of the briefs I am handed come from people that leave a lot to be desired when it comes to writing skills.

That was nearly twenty years ago and I still remember having the conversation. Brace yourselves because this is where I am going to upset a lot of public relations people.

Sadly, many (not all) public relations representatives suck at writing press releases for bands and shows. It isn't that they are horrible technical writers; the problem is that many of them do not communicate effectively with the media, opting to create hype and come across as "selling" an idea instead of explaining why the client is newsworthy. So what can you do to make sure your band's press releases give you the best chance of getting coverage?

The inner workings of a newsroom...

To understand how to write a better press release for your band and shows, you first need to have a working knowledge of what goes on in a newsroom. When you call a television news station or a newspaper, more often than not an assignment editor answers your call. The job of an assignment editor is to sort through all potential news stories, decide which stories will be covered, and then assign each story to the reporter best suited to cover that particular topic. If the media outlet you are attempting to contact has an entertainment editor, the assignment editor will probably pass your information to that individual and let them decide whether or not to cover it.

So, to put this in more relatable (Ghostbuster) terms, the assignment/entertainment editors are the Gatekeepers and your press release is the Keymaster. Got that? I hope so because there is more to know.

Due to issues with the economy, the increased automation in the radio industry, and something referred to as "hub and spoking" the news, many radio stations in small and medium sized markets have downsized their news departments to just one person. Why is that important to you when you are trying to get coverage for your band? Because that means you are likely sending your press releases and information to a tired and overworked (and sometimes cranky) news director. It sounds very doom-and-gloom but this actually works to your advantage if you know what the hell you are doing.

Drop the sales pitch and concentrate on being newsworthy...

There are two major theories when it comes to the tone of how a press release is written. One of them is written to increase hype and sell somebody on the idea of covering the subject while the other is subtler and explores how newsworthy the subject is.

The sales pitch-style releases are usually pretty obnoxious. Many of them talk about your band like you are the second coming of U2 while attempting to convince the Gatekeeper that a reporter MUST be at the show or risk missing out on a piece of music history. But there is a massive problem with this approach: entertainment journalists know your band isn't that good. I know that comment probably stings your pride but it is the truth. It is kind of like when some of you are trying to book a show at a venue and you tell the booking manager about how sure you are that the place will be at capacity for the show when you know damn well that won't be the case. The booking managers hear the sales pitch...all...the...time. Entertainment reporters are in the exact same situation. They get show announcement after show announcement talking about how great a band is and see the hype for what it really is.

So instead of buying into the hype, journalists want to know what makes you "newsworthy." Your press release needs to explain to them what it is about you and your show that makes you different from the thousands of other bands competing for that newspaper space or radio or television time.

What reaches the standard of being "newsworthy" depends on a number of variables. One thing you have to take into consideration is the size of the media market in which you are seeking coverage. The standard is much higher in a larger city than it is in a small town where less is typically happening on a day-to-day basis. What is front-page material in Small-town, Wyoming might never see coverage in Los Angeles or Nashville. Why? Because your band is competing for coverage against every other band in that area as well as every other potential news and sports story. You have to keep in mind that there is only so much newspaper space and radio and television time to go around.

This is why having a good press release writer on your side is so damn important, regardless of whether you are writing it yourself or having a public relations firm write it for you. The good press release writers will sit down and learn everything about you and find something that each media outlet will find interesting. You know how one of the goals of most bands should be to know and understand their audience and how to communicate with them? Good press release writers know their audiences are the assignment and entertainment editors and write to capture their interest.

The power of copy and paste...

I should be making you pay large sums of money for this tip because it is one of my bread-and-butter press release tactics. Instead of sending traditional press releases about your band or show, send out a prewritten news story disguised as a press release.

Most newsrooms, regardless of market size or medium, are severely understaffed and overworked. They just don't have enough people to write about every single thing they want to cover. If you can hone your writing skills to the media outlets' standards and write a news story like they would, there is a very real possibility that they will copy and paste your press release and put it directly into the paper. This is a fairly common practice in many newsrooms. They do it with press releases from politicians as well as with stories that come from wire services like the Associated Press.

If you are going to employ this tactic when sending something to a newspaper, make sure it is no longer than one page and try to cram all of your most important details into the first paragraph or two. The reason is because the newspaper's layout department might need something small to fill in a gap on one of the pages. If they snag your story and clip off most of it, you want to be sure the most important information is still intact. Don't get flowery with your writing. Keep it simple and be efficient in your word usage.

If you are sending something like this to a radio station, be certain it is no longer than five lines. Scripts for news stories in radio have to be kept extremely short because they don't have much time on the air. If it takes longer than thirty seconds for you to read aloud (at a brisk pace), then you need to cut stuff out. Even though this sounds very simple to write, you will find it is extremely difficult to do on a high level.

Be aware of news cycles...

Remember how I mentioned that newspapers are limited in the space they can dedicate to news coverage each day and how the same problem applies to radio and television stations in the form of time? It is important to always remember that because it means some days are more difficult than others to get a story about your band or show past the Gatekeeper and into the news.

It pays to not be oblivious to things going on around you. If you are getting ready to send out a release and you know that the Winter Storm of the Century is going to hit in two days, hold on to the release until after things quiet down. If a local professional sports team just won a championship or is about to go to one, wait until everything related to it passes before sending the release. Think about it: major events, whether they are on a national or local level, will receive in-depth coverage that will suck up a lot of space in the newspaper and a lot of time on radio and television. News outlets look for every possible angle on stories so even a sixty-minute newscast can be left with only a little bit of time if they are dedicating the first fifteen minutes to a major story. And don't forget they still have to do weather two or three times as well as sports and run commercials. That time can be extremely hard to get so wait until these kinds of things are done before sending the release.

There is a lot to be said about having access to somebody capable of writing a killer press release. And, yes, writing press releases IS a service we offer at Rocket to the Stars. If you are writing your own releases, be sure to keep a lot of this stuff in mind. If you are paying a PR representative to write them for you, make certain they are following these tips. Remember: They work for you. Not the other way around.

Three Common PR Mistakes
Your Band Must Avoid

Wade Sutton, Rocket to the Stars

As I was putting the finishing touches on a previous develop-ment article, I couldn't help but go back and look over some of the comments from Beaver County Times entertainment editor Scott Tady. One of the stories he relayed to me struck a chord.

The story I am referring to is Tady's telling of having to track down a photograph of a band he was writing an article about. The short version is that Scott was writing a piece on a band that was part of an upcoming doubleheader in Pittsburgh. Scott wrote the story and contacted the band because he needed a photograph for the article. When the band failed to get back to him, Scott attempted to reach the band's publicist. The publicist, like the band, also failed to send the photograph. Scott was left with few choices and ulti-mately decided to run the story...with a photograph of the other band set to perform in that show.

I'm going to tell you something very disheartening: This sort of thing happens more often than many of you would believe. I find it truly amazing that so many bands do not comprehend how quickly inadequate public relations and media representa-tion can ruin their reputation in media circles and how much it can hold them back from advancing in their careers. I am com-pletely sympathetic of bands that don't have the money to hire the proper representation but, if that is the position you are in, it is vital that you give this part of your music business the atten-tion it deserves.

I am going to tell you three TRUE stories that I have had to deal with in just the past few weeks. Some involve bands that currently have no public relations or media representation while others are currently under contract with firms. This is the kind of stuff that goes on behind the scenes...

Story #1...

Just a few weeks ago, I reached out to a singer I was interested in covering for one of my in-depth artist interviews. The artist is very talented and was in the process of wrapping up a tour. My initial contact with her was via Twitter and she appeared to be genuinely enthusiastic in her responses. I requested her e-mail address so I could send her a standard form I give all artists prior to one of my interviews.

Understand that the form I send them includes a section explaining that Rocket's long-form interviews are typically conducted via Skype. I'm not going to go into many specifics here but being able to see the person I am interviewing is an important part of my interview methodology. A person's mannerisms, body language, and facial expressions are all indicators of when I should increase pressure or ease up during certain lines of questions. I take the interview process so seriously because doing so leads to the wonderful artist interviews published by Rocket to the Stars. It is a matter of maintaining a standard with my readers in mind.

Back to the story. So I sent that form to the e-mail address provided to me by the artist. Four days later, I received a response from the public relations firm representing the artist. It said that she had agreed to the terms of the interview and wanted to set up a time to conduct it but, near the end of the e-mail, the public relations representative includes a brief comment informing me that the interview would be done by telephone instead of utilizing Skype.

"Huh? That isn't how this works," I thought to myself. I sent a very polite response to the public relations representative explaining that doing the interview on Skype was part of Rocket's policy for conducting and writing our artist interviews. I also explained the reasons for the process being what it was and even provided them with links to previous artist interviews on our site so they could see what type of article I was aiming to write about their client. They later responded saying they felt it would be better to do the interview by phone and "suggested" times that would be good for them to conduct the interview.

I went to Twitter and contacted the artist directly in an attempt to figure out what the hell was going on and I asked her if there was a specific reason she didn't want to do the interview on Skype. She responded to my inquiry and said that she was more than willing to do the interview in that manner and was confused by the e-mails I was receiving from her public relations representative. I suggested we set up a time and day to do the Skype interview (I wanted to get the interview posted because I had other stories I needed to work on) and she suddenly became very hesitant.

That was all I needed to know. I immediately pulled the plug on the interview. I knew one of two things was happening: either there was a complete lack of communication between the artist and the public relations representative or the artist, for what ever reason, did not want to do the Skype interview and wasn't being honest with me when we spoke about it. The interview never happened.

Journalists have more important things to do than waste time trying to sort through this kind of mess. Getting one story from an artist while their PR crew is saying the exact opposite is unprofessional and makes it very difficult for media to take you seriously. It also makes us not want to cover you.

Story #2...

If you, your public relations representative, or your band's manager decides to contact the media hoping to get coverage for your show, do not send one of those stupid e-mails pretending to be a fan suggesting the media outlet "check out this totally awesome local band." You think you are being slick but an experienced journalist, even one working in a small town, will sniff that out from a mile away. Do you want to know why we are so good at detecting that kind of BS? Because it happens so often. It happens in music news and it runs rampant in political news coverage.

It was just last week that somebody e-mailed me suggesting I watch a YouTube of some band from New York City. The author of the e-mail went on to say they thought the band had potential and he just happened to think of Rocket to the Stars (JOY!) and he thought I might be interested in doing an interview with the band.

Of course, he just happened to have links to their YouTube videos and website.

"Seriously?" I groaned.

I immediately responded to the e-mail asking if the author was the band's manager. Sure enough that ended up being the case. I received a message from the guy about ten minutes later admitting that he was their manager.

I'm going to give you a pro tip: If the artist or band in question is NEWSWORTHY, journalists do not care if it is a member of the band, a manager, or a fan contacting us with the tip. If you are a member of the band, a public relations representative, or a manger pulling double duty, please, just say so from the beginning. We are going to find out and it will make you look tacky and unprofessional.

And if you do feel you need to pretend to be somebody else, that act probably isn't newsworthy enough for coverage to begin with.

Story #3...

If there is any one-lesson artists take from this article, I hope it will be this: Journalists contacting you for interviews are usually working on some sort of deadline. I know of several instances in which journalists and entertainment writers decided to drop an interview with an artist because it would take so long for the performer to get back to them. This problem is not exclusive to the music industry. It happens in politics, with community events, and several other areas of news coverage.

You have to understand that reporters live and die by their ability to meet deadlines and uncover stories before their competition. So when a reporter suddenly seems less interested in interviewing you and writing about your band, don't start criticizing and saying nasty things about them on social media. More often than not those interviews are getting dropped because you have a pattern of waiting three days to respond to the journalist's inquiries. Once that pattern carries out over the course of three e-mails, the reporter has already blown more than a week trying to set up the interview and get the information he or she needs.

I had this happen with three different artists... just last week. Most reporters do not have time to deal with this kind of thing because they have deadlines they have to meet to keep their jobs. They have editors breathing down their neck to get things done. I don't have an editor standing over me at Rocket to the Stars but I still maintain self-imposed deadlines to guarantee new content is being posted on a regular basis.

And one more pro tip to close this thing out: If a reporter is interested in covering you, they are probably watching you on social media. So when they wait three days for you to respond to an e-mail while seeing you post on Facebook every twenty minutes, well, they are probably going to drop you in favor of covering somebody else.

And the chances of them ever covering you again are slim.

CHAPTER 6

Management

Music Managers (Part 1)

Rick Barker, Music Industry Blueprint's "25 Minutes From Nashville"

I get a lot of questions concerning managers. When should you get a manager? How to pick up a manager? What makes a good manager? So what I'd look to do is take a few of these segments and talk to you, in detail about the management side of things.

As many of you know, and its very well documented, when Taylor chose me as her manager, I didn't have any previous major management experience. Basically I had worked with a few unsigned artists and I had these goofy ideas, but going to school for a degree in management or anything like that, I did not have. What I thought a manager did turned out to be completely different than what a manager actually does. So I am going to share all of that with you.

When determining if you should have a manager, most people don't have things to manage at that particular point in time and they are not generating enough revenue to be able to afford to pay their manager. That's what makes it tough, because you are the only client that a manager has and you are not generating any income for that manager to survive. You don't necessarily know how much time they are going to spend on you. If you get the fortunate ability to be with a manager who is at a management company, and has a couple of other artists who are making money and they are willing to take you on as an artist, that can be very beneficial but it also means that, because you are not the one generating the majority of the revenue, you may not be getting the attention that you feel you deserve. So there is a Catch-22 in having a successful manager take you on early in your career.

I think, first and foremost, you need to understand the role of a manager. A manager's role, in my opinion and some people will differ with this and that's okay, is to teach, advise, and guide. It is not to do everything for you and, trust me, I have made the mistake of doing everything for my artist. It created little monsters. So my role as Taylor's manager was not only to teach Taylor, but also to help execute. I was the go-between for her and the label, and when we were on site, between her and her tour manager, her and her band.

She dealt specifically with her business manager and attorney. I wasn't the go-between there. I was a go-between with the booking agent. My job was to filter all these offers that would come in and decide which ones were the right ones to present to her and her family. At the time, not every offer was the right thing so I was able to weed that out and not bother them with those things. Because she was a young artist, my responsibility was making sure she was being put in situations where she could succeed. Never putting the artist in a position for them to fail. Unfortunately, a lot of those things you can't control but you've got to do your best job possible to make sure that every light or every situation that you put your artist into allows them to succeed and see some level of success.

I was also the go-between with her merchandise company and I was involved in helping with the creation. I was involved in her logistics, her day-to-day scheduling, calendar and things like that. So you can basically figure it out where you are. If you have a lot of those things that I just mentioned going on in your career right now, it would be very smart to grab yourself a manager.

Now, what do you want to look for in a manager? First off, I think you need to find someone who is passionate about you. I was very passionate about Taylor. I believed in her vision. I believed in her plans. So find someone who is passionate about you. Now, I have terrible organizational skills. I would find someone who has great organizational skills. I was blessed to be able to put together a team of people. I never build a team of people just like me. I built a team of people who had skills that I didn't have which made me better. So if you can find someone who is passionate about you and is very organized, well, that helps.

I think right now that you need to find someone who understands the Internet and understands that times have changed. I think you need to find someone that you trust, that can jump your ass if they need to, who can get on you and make you work knowing that they respect you and they trust you. Too often artists tend to associate themselves with, I call them "yes" people. That can be very dangerous. So you need to make sure that your manager is someone you trust.

Your manager doesn't necessarily have to come from the music business but they should be studying the music business. They should understand the nuances of the music business. I think that they should be great communicators because they're basically representing you. They are a direct reflection of you so if they don't present themselves in a great way, then I don't know if that's who you want representing your business. You should find someone who doesn't know it all. You should find someone who is willing to ask questions and make things better on your behalf.

That was one of the great things about my situation with managing Taylor, that I wasn't afraid to say, "You know what? I don't know the answer to that but give me 24 hours and I will find out." I also allied myself with a lot of people that I could do great things for and help so they would pick up when I would call so I could get the answers to those questions. So create great alliances with people. There are some fantastic books out there right now; David Hooper's book "The Six Figure Musician." I remember picking up

Donald Passman's book just to learn the lingo, to carry on a conversation with someone, and at least get through that conversation so I could go and research.

Google is a valuable tool nowadays. Bob Baker has some great books. There are a lot of great resources out there. Make sure your manager is keeping up to date on the changes of what's happening and, honestly, if you are in a position to be able to compensate your manager in some way, shape, or form, even if you are not making revenue yourself, I would do that. The reason I would do that is because this person is working every day on your behalf and it could be years, if ever, that you make a dime in the traditional way that they would even see a penny from that.

So find somebody, like I said, they don't have to solely survive on you making it right now or else you are getting put into situations that won't help you grow as an artist. And I speak on that from experience. Find someone that is a go-getter and is not afraid to think outside of the box. More opportunities were created for Taylor and myself because we thought differently. You know a lot of people think that you need to find that person who has done it before. No! But you need to find that person who is willing to do it, if that makes any sense. I was willing to try anything and I was willing to try it out first myself and put it through the test before I brought my artist into the situation.

I guess what I am trying to say is don't go to the same places that everyone else is going. It's crowded there. Try to create your own space. That's what I did with the seven free songs, that's what I did with Taylor and I doing the meet and greets. We created our own spaces because we knew it wasn't going to be crowded and, in the end, it was tremendous the way that these things worked.

So start thinking, who do you know that would like to be in the music business? Who do you know that's super sharp? Whose opinion do you trust and who do you think will be honest with you? Start making yourself a list and start asking them if they would like to be a part of your team. You don't even have to call it "manager" in the beginning. Just let them know you are putting a team together and you would like them to be a part of your team and see if they have the opportunity to work themselves in that role.

That's kind of how it happened with me. I was still working for the record company and Taylor had some questions. She wanted to learn the radio. They came down. We spent some time together. I started taking on a little bit more responsibility all the time and the next thing you know, her family was calling and asking if I would like to be her manager. So I kind of worked myself into that position and it wasn't the first time that they met me they said, "Hey, Rick's the perfect guy for this". So work yourself into that role.

If you are reading this and you'd like to be a manager, work yourself into that role. Find yourself a band that you believe in and say, "Hey, I'd like to help you get better. I would like to help you achieve your dreams. I think I can be a very valuable part of your team," and work yourself into that situation."

Music Managers (Part 2)

Rick Barker, Music Industry Blueprint's "25 Minutes From Nashville"

I'm actually heading in to SAE Institute, which has been known as a great audio engineering college. They have 50 campuses throughout the world in 25 countries. They recently have started a music business program where you can get an Associate's degree in like 16 months and I have been asked to teach the Entertainment Marketing class. I am very excited about that.

I always tell people the best way to learn how to be a manager is to be a manager. You want to know what it is like? Get in and do it. So what I'm actually going to be able to do, which is awesome, is take some of my Blueprint clients and let them be clients for the students. And a good part of their grade is going to be what they actually did with an artist. I am very excited about that. Practical experience, we love it!

I was looking at the first part of the Music Managers series and I thought, "What is it that I would be looking for if I were to manage an artist today? What are the things that would attract me? What are some of the things and advice that I could give an artist or their family on the things they should be doing right now if they want to attract the manager?"

As we discussed in the last section, a manager only gets paid if you're getting paid. So trying to seek out and get an experienced manager in the beginning, when you're not generating an income, it's going to be very hard. It is not impossible. Nothing is impossible but it is very hard.

So you want to make yourself as attractive to this person, to this potential manager, as you possibly can. What I would be looking for is an artist who has a great work ethic. They just don't talk about what they are going to do. They are actually doing it to the point that I could look on social media and see that they are engaging their fan base, that I can see that they are touring, that they are performing, and that they are getting better. Remember, I don't care about how pretty you are or how great you sound. Thousands and thousands of people just like that are all over the place. I am looking for that rare person.

All of the iconic superstar artists are also great business people. So I am also going to be looking for someone who understands and treats it like a business. I want to make sure that somebody is working every day, I want to make sure that I find someone who isn't afraid to get their hands dirty. Somebody not looking for their manager to do all the work. I also think that I would probably "date" for a little while. I want to see how that artist handles the bad times. Not just the good times. The thing that sucks the most about being a manager is when everything is going great, the artist or the label get all the credit. But when it's going badly, it always falls back to the manager. And that's just wrong but, hey, that's part of the business. And that's one of the things you need to expect if you plan on being a manager.

But I want to see how this artist handles adversity. I want to see how this artist handles instruction. I want to see how this artist reacts when things don't go right at a gig. I want to see how this artist reacts when they read some negative press. Before, I would find myself falling in love with the music first and then working my tail off on behalf of the artist. This time around, I want to see the true colors of the artist. And, a lot of times, you don't get to see that for a while.

So I also think that for young artists and parents, there's no need to jump into a contract real quickly. Let the managers prove themselves to you because it's a relationship. You are "dating." That's why I like the process, or the thought of, possibly "dating" a manager first. Keep in mind that if anything comes from the date the manager generates for you income-wise, that manager is entitled to whatever percentage that you guys agreed upon. I just don't want anyone getting locked into a long-term engagement. I would also get all of the artists that I decide to take on long term under contract.

I've done the handshake deal before and that has come back to bite me. Everyone has great intentions but whenever there's money or intention involved, you should always have a contract. If they don't want to sign a contract with you, they are probably not the right artist that you want to be involved with manager-wise.

Also, if you are an artist signing the contract, make sure that the sunset clause works with you turning that on and make sure that it's realistic. So if somebody is with you for three months and their contract states that they have a five-year sunset on you, which are bull. So really make sure that the things are really proportionate there.

Another thing in looking for an artist is you want to make sure that this artist understands time management. A lot of times they tend to get overwhelmed and that can be taught. And that's one of the things that we are really trying to focus on inside the Music Industry Blueprint. I'm preparing the artists for their time management. Let me watch them get overwhelmed right now and try to help them out. And it's cute. I mean, it's part of life.

But it also shows me when they pick up the phone and they call and say, look, it's not going well right now. What do I do? That is the type of artist I want to work with. I want to work with someone who can be honest. I want someone to be able to show me their faults because we can help them when they show their faults. So often, artists try to show only the good side.

Parents are the worst at this. All they want to do is to tell you how great their kid is. Advice to parents: Stop telling us how great your kid is. We will determine that for ourselves. And remember that, if your child is a minor, the label is also signing you. So if you are a pain in the ass, then your kid probably won't get signed because the labels won't want to deal with you.

If you are an artist, show me that you are a hard worker. Show me that you are consistently doing the things you need to do to move your career forward. Show me that you put in the initiative. Show me that you are out there busting your hump every day to move your career forward.

If you are a manager, what kind of artist should you be looking for? Work ethic, work ethic, honesty, and integrity. That's just my little bit of advice to you.

Music Managers (Part 3)

Rick Barker, Music Industry Blueprint's "25 Minutes From Nashville"

I have become an expert in finding experts. I have 25 years of knowledge and experience, which I like, because you can't buy knowledge and experience... but you can rent it. You can lease it if you find the right people. So, this final part is about the "Momager" and the "Dadager." The parent managers.

Most of the time, almost 99% of the time, you are your child's first manager and a lot of the foundation that you set up will determine whether they make it or not. I have watched very talented kids completely fall apart because their parents mismanaged them and it's not because a parent would purposely ever do anything to harm their child. I know, I am a parent. It's because they didn't know any better because there wasn't a place where they could get information. They were so into how great they thought their kid was that they took bad information and if you are going to act as a manager for your kid, you have to learn some things.

There are some things that I am going to say that are going to probably piss you off and if they piss you off it's because you are THAT parent. So you can either go to therapy or shoot me an e-mail. Another thing I want to say, and I say this at every event that I speak at live, is that you shouldn't go into panic mode if I say some things that you have been doing wrong. You are not supposed to know these things. You are parents for goodness sakes. Most of you are running a house; you have a career and have more than one kid. You are trying to do everything you can to make sure all your kids are getting taken care of. So don't get down on yourself if I say some things and you are like, "Crap, I am the one who did that." Fix it.

If you are the one having to convince your kid to write, to perform, to sing, to do all these things they are not ready for the business side of things so thank them for showing you they are not ready and don't spend a fortune trying to force them to get ready. Let them be kids. They've only got one chance at being a kid. If when they come home every day and they are like I want to play my guitar, I want to write songs, or I want to sing, nurture and guide that. Make sure that you start investing in better vocal lessons and better instrument lessons and better education for the music business, but if they are not excited about doing it every day, don't force them to do it.

Secondly, just because your kid wins a contest in your local town does not mean that you are ready to come to Nashville and hire Carrie Underwood's band and go on radio tour. It means your kid won a contest. See if they can win the next contest and the next contest and, if that is the case, then you want to get them with better vocal coaches and performance coaches and people who can help guide their career so you can keep building that. More often than not one of your friends will say, "Oh my gosh, your kid should be on the radio," and you go, "Oh my gosh, they should be on the radio." And the next thing you know, you are chasing a dream and you haven't given your kid the tools to succeed. You are just throwing money at something and, when it doesn't happen, do you know how it makes a 16-year-old kid feel having gone through grandma's savings so the parents could help them live this dream? I have watched it. It devastates kids. I have watched kids need therapy because of it. It's a lot of pressure to put on a kid.

If you as a parent were a singer or a songwriter or in a band, make sure your kids are doing this for them and not you. Make sure you are pushing them and help guide them for THEIR career and not the career that you wish YOU had. If you get the opportunity to be around professionals, don't tell us how great your kid is. We will determine that for our self. We are professionals. That's what we do. Especially if we are the ones who want to make an investment in that kid.

Remember, if your child is a minor the label is also signing you. So don't be the thing that causes your kids not to get that opportunity. Sit down, be quiet, and support your kid... rock on. If it's supposed to happen, it's supposed to happen. Outside of Disney and Nickelodeon, we are not set up for children. There is a reason for it; because they are kids. Because we are in an adult business, we play with adult money, and we want people who can treat it that way. That's who we are going to put in charge of the bank account. So do everything you can to help your kid.

Let them get to their teens. Nine- and ten-year-olds having to just truck ride it out and do this every day; I am not a fan of that at all. Let them be kids but, like I said, if you have got that talented teenager, there are things you need to do. You want to start making sure that they are getting trained vocally. I will compare it to soccer. I coached soccer for a long time. Your kid was playing at the YMCA and everything was fun and then you realized your kid has some talent. So they maybe played for a club team and that cost a bit more money, the training costs a little bit more because the coaches are better. There is travel involved so it's starting to get really expensive and then, all of a sudden, your kid's really, really killing it and doing fantastic and they end up in the Olympic development program. Now that gets even more expensive because the coaching is getting better, there is more travel, and there is more time being spent with the coaches.

We see that as being okay in sports but for some reason, we don't see that as being okay in the music business. We are afraid to pay for coaching. We are afraid to pay for people's expertise and their knowledge. We will pay a vocal coach $300 an hour but you won't pay a coach $150 an hour who could actually make the bigger difference in their career. So I want you to start reevaluating things. I want you to start spending your money wisely. I want you to sit down and say, "Okay, let's get some songs critiqued the right way before we go in and record them. Let's get it critiqued by an actual songwriter that's had a hit." Those options are available. There are a lot of things that you could be doing as a parent and, if you start making the right decisions now, you will have a better relationship with your kid and you are going to save money.

We need that next batch of stars to get trained earlier rather than later so they can have careers and you, as a parent, have the ability to get that education now and set them up the right way. I am excited. Everyone always asks me, "Hey, are your kids in the music business?" and I am like, "Heck, no. I am going to get them in the management."

I am going to get them into graphic design and I am going to get them in those other areas of the music business because it's hard to be an artist. There is a lot of pressure and it takes a special person to handle that kind of pressure. If your kid is super shy and they are timid, don't keep putting them up on stage until they are ready.

Sometimes the reason these kids are getting bullied is because of the things that their parents are doing when they are around other kids. And it's because you are putting stuff up on YouTube way too early. Your kids need to be the best friends and cool friends with everybody in school. They don't need to always brag about all the contests that they are doing or the contests that they are winning, especially if they are in a public school.

Kids look for reasons to get on other kids. Don't have them become that kid that everybody picks on and you be the one who caused it. You know what I am saying? I hope you understand and if you don't, call me. Your kid is no better than any other kid and if you err on the side of humility and be humble and gracious and if people say, "Hey, I heard you were in a contest," tell them, "You know what? I was blessed to be able to perform this week and it was awesome. Hey, how was your weekend?" It goes back to that conversation thing. It will protect them.

CHAPTER 7

How To....

How to Get Sponsorships For Your Live Shows

Wade Sutton, Rocket to the Stars

Many singers and bands not achieving their desired level of success are being held back not by a lack of talent, but rather their lack of commitment to the business side of their act.

It can't be helped, really. As singers and musicians, many of you were first drawn to the stage because of the rush of emotions that comes with being the center of attention while rocking out in front of a bunch of screaming fans. So many of you spend a great many years learning to sing, practicing your instrument, working (hopefully) on your songwriting skills, and fantasizing about that day you get noticed by a label.

Unfortunately a lot of singers and bands have little or zero business sense and they are losing money because of it. It is a popular question asked by a lot of performers. They want to know how they can get sponsors for their shows. Many are clueless as to how to go about getting sponsors, instead relying on whatever they make at the door or from selling merchandise to fund what they do. And, yes, it does require quite a bit of work and effort (if you want to do it well) but it is a source of income that so many miss out on.

First things first...

We have always had a rule at Rocket to the Stars: Don't wing it. That applies to what you do on the business side of your music just as much as what you do when you are on stage performing. You need a plan. The plan gives you guidance. It is your map that points you in the right direction, step by step.

Identify your potential revenue sources...

Rule #1: You can't sell an idea to a sponsor if you don't know exactly what it is that you are selling.

A sponsor will not cut you a check if you can't tell them what they are sponsoring. Are they sponsoring your live shows? Are they sponsoring something on your website? What are they getting out of the deal? It isn't up to them to determine that. It is up to YOU to figure that out. In the eyes of the business thinking about sponsoring you, this is not charity; it is advertising. Some possibilities for revenue sources that nearly every band has available to them...

1. Sponsoring your live shows. Selling naming rights is a huge deal in the media right now. If you can think of something, tangible or not, you can probably find somebody out there willing to pay you to have their name applied to it. Nearly every sports stadium and arena has some corporate name splashed across it (Heinz Field, Quicken Loans Arena, etc.). Radio stations are even selling naming rights to the very studios they broadcast from (Westgate Plaza Studios) and have their jocks and talk show hosts always refer to the studio on the air by that purchased name. It is exposure for the sponsor's name and brand, whether it be seen or heard. How does it work with your live shows? Easy. "Chivas Regal Presents: Feline Funk Live In Concert."

2. Ads on your website. There are so many reasons for a singer or band to have their own website. Not a fan page on Facebook. Not a page on Reverbnation. I'm talking about an actual website. Not only does it serve as the center of operations for everything you do when it comes to marketing and publicity, it is also a source of revenue. Ever read our very first blog talking about bands approaching the media when trying to get coverage for a show? I explained in that piece that every square inch of a newspaper has an actual monetary value assigned to it, which is determined, in part, by the newspaper's readership numbers. The same concept applies to your website. The more visitors to your website each month, the more money you can charge for naming rights (as the name of your live show sponsor will also have their name plastered all over your site) as well as other sponsors looking to be included on your page.

3. Your YouTube channel. This is a great source for some extra revenue if you or somebody you know possesses video editing skills. Put together a short promotional video plugging your upcoming shows or tour and splash your sponsors' names all over it. Then e-mail blast the video to fans who signed up for your e-mail list and post the link for the video all over your social media pages. And if you really want to impress your sponsors, have the promo be preceded by a short video of you sending out a sincere and heartfelt thank you to your sponsors...and be sure to name them in the message.
   Don't forget to tweet the link to those sponsors, too.

4. Giveaways before the show and contests during the show. Sponsors LOVE when people personally talk about and endorse their products and you have plenty of opportunities to do this. Is there a way you can incorporate your sponsor's product into a ticket contest in the weeks leading up to the show? Do the contests on social media and make sure videos and pictures are involved so their product is visible. And you can do the same thing with contests during your show. See if the sponsor will give you some samples of their product or a gift card for their business. Another reason why this is such a

great idea: It gives you time to talk to and interact with your fans during a show. They will love it!

5. On your tickets and merchandise. Earlier I mentioned "Chivas Regal Presents: Feline Funk Live In Concert." If you are having paper tickets printed for pre-sale or for at the door, put your sponsor's name and logo on the ticket. That ticket has monetary advertising value. Don't let it go to waste. Are you lining up a ten-show mini-tour during which you will be selling merchandise? Businesses crave opportunities to have their name and logo printed on the back of t-shirts because it turns your fans into walking billboards. Selling CDs at shows? That is another place you can place a logo.

6. Product placement. Go back and look at some of the pictures currently posted on your website. Are you holding a Gibson guitar? Singing into a Sennheiser microphone? Wearing an outfit you purchased at Buckle? Sitting in front of your Mac? If so, the only difference between product placement advertising and what you are doing now is you aren't currently getting paid for it. Change that! Add those companies to your list of potential sponsors. Plan to show them the pictures that could include their products being used!

Now let's talk numbers...

Rule #2: The amount of money you will be able to ask for when approaching somebody for a sponsorship is determined by your "reach."

Allow me to explain the concept of "reach." Many of you trying to make it in the music industry have probably heard of something in the radio business known as Arbitron. Arbitron is a service many radio stations subscribe to (yes, radio stations pay for this). Arbitron mails "diaries" to people all over and asks them to write down what radio stations they listen at various times. The diaries are eventually returned, Arbitron compiles all of the data, applies some top-secret formula and, POOF, they come up with a list of how many people are listening to each station in every media market. Those lists are the "ratings" for the stations. The higher the station's ratings, the more "reach" it has, the more money it can get in the form of sponsorships. A very similar process takes place with television in the form of Nielsen ratings. For print media, newspapers and magazines, "reach" is determined by circulation (subscriptions and news stand sales).

Got it? Okay. Remember when we talked about identifying your revenue sources? We mentioned a number of them, including your website, your e-mail lists, social media, YouTube, and your live shows. All of those facets of your music business help determine your act's "reach" and how much money you should be asking for when seeking sponsorships. The end result of all of this is a great indicator of the strength of your brand.

Time to roll up the sleeves and start looking at the numbers you will need to show potential advertisers. Understand that your chances of getting somebody to agree to sponsor your act are much higher if you can show them hard numbers (even if the numbers aren't as high as you would like) than by not providing the numbers and hoping they simply like you enough to open their checkbook for you. The figures you will want to be able to provide them include the following:

1. How many monthly visitors and page views do you have on your website?*
2. How many subscribers do you have to your website's e-mail list?
3. What is the average attendance at your live shows?
4. How many followers and likes do you have on social media, including Twitter, Facebook, and Instagram?
5. How many views do you have on your YouTube channel?

*Concerning #1.** If you do have a website and are not paying a service to track the traffic on your website, it is time to start. Google Analytics is free and there are other good services out there for as little as five dollars per month. Simply having those numbers will make you look considerably more professional when going to businesses for sponsorships. If you don't have a website, you are missing out on one of the biggest revenue generators for your music business. Stop looking at a website as a "cost" and realize it is an "investment" that pays huge dividends.

Have all those numbers ready to go? Good. Set them aside because now we have to start thinking about demographics.

Rule #3: Singers and bands who don't bother trying to identify their demographic are like being behind the wheel at night with no headlights.

Demographics play a huge role in what you do as an act. Who is in your crowd? How old are they? Is your crowd predominately male, female, or a healthy mix of the two? What is the general cultural background of your audience? Do they typically have a common interest that is drawing them to your shows?

Why is this important? Because if you can figure out who your audience is, you can figure out what they spend their money on. And if you know what they are buying, you will know EXACTLY what businesses to go to for sponsorships.

This is one of the good things about Facebook fan pages because there is a button near the top of the screen that says, "View Insights." Click on it and hit the "People" tab. It gives you a breakdown of all the Facebook users liking your page. There is information on the male-to-female ratio, an age breakdown, and it tells you exactly where all of those people live.

Rule #4: Keep your sales proposal as simple as possible. It makes it easier for businesses to understand and leaves less room for you to make a mistake. One of the best ways to go about putting this proposal together is to break it up into three pages.

First page: This is essentially a cover letter. Introduce yourself and your act and provide the prospective client some very basic background information on your act. Yes, you are looking for businesses willing to sponsor your show but that is NOT how you will present it in this letter. Want you want to do is appeal to their business sense. Explain that you are looking to help them market their business and product to potential customers (your audience). This page should include your band's logo at the top along with contact information, including your website URL (NOT your Reverbnation or Facebook pages). Make it a point to mention that your audience's demographics are very similar to their own.

Second page: Here is where you explain what you are offering to the target business (access to your audience and fans) and SHOWING them your "reach." Include a small graph or chart that lays out the number of hits-per-month on your website (include numbers for the past three months to keep it current), the number of people following you on Twitter, Facebook, and other social media, the number of views on your YouTube channel, average attendance at your live shows, and how many people are subscribed to your e-mail list. If you can pull it off, include a picture from your website or one of your shows in which that business' product or logo is visible.

Third page: This is the page that lays out exactly what businesses get for sponsoring you and your show. This can get a little tricky and sometimes requires flexibility on your part. You need to put together several packages (aka "tiers") to give businesses two or three buy-in options. Your biggest (and most expensive) option should include everything you can make available: Banners at all live shows that are part of the package, ads on your website, mentions on social media and YouTube, mentions and links to their websites when you send out e-mails to your subscribers, and naming rights to your shows (i.e.: "Chivas Regal Presents: Feline Funk, Live In Concert").

Why multiple buy-in options for sponsorships? A lot of reasons. Some businesses might not have enough money freed up in their budget to go all out and do everything they can with you. Also, some businesses might tend to go for the lower option until they can develop a good working relationship with you and your band. Keep in mind that the business that gives you only a little bit of money today could be your biggest source of advertising revenue in the future. That is why it is important to create and foster those relationships over time. What it all comes down to is this: Make it as easy as possible for a business to give you their money!

The question that is ALWAYS asked: How much should I charge for sponsorships? There is no definitive answer to this as what every singer and band offers varies. However there is something very important to keep in mind. As artists, you pour a ton of time and energy into your work. You are extremely proud of what you do and what you create. As a result, singers and bands tend to overvalue their product when trying to decide how much money to ask for in return for a sponsorship. This is very common for new people getting into all types of business. Whatever you initially plan to charge for sponsorships will probably be a little bit too high and you will likely have to come down some (be flexible). When the day ends, you do not determine the value of your sponsorship packages... your advertisers set the value.

Rule #5: Don't approach random businesses. Get the most out of your time and energy by going to businesses that target the same people making up your audience.

Hopefully you thought about your demographics because now it is time to take the proposal to those businesses. Do it in person. Do...not...e-mail...them. Going to the business and speaking face-to-face has a much greater impact and gives the prospective advertiser an opportunity to get to know you on a personal level. Be friendly and be service-oriented. Understand that somebody thinking about giving you money for a sponsorship is a customer and must be treated as such. They might come back with some kind of counter-proposal or talk to you about a special need or request. It is up to you to decide whether or not to meet them half way.

Something to think about: For many businesses, the best time to approach them about a sponsorship is around the middle of Fall. That is because a lot of businesses are putting together their budgets for the following calendar year at that time and a big chunk of those budgets include advertising. Once that budget window closes, many businesses become tightfisted when it comes to expenditures. If you miss that seasonal window, shoot for the third week of the month. It is around that time that many businesses have a general idea whether they are ahead of or behind monthly projections. If you catch them in a good month, you will give yourself a better chance of convincing them to throw some money your way.

I know this is a lot of work but here is the best part: Once you do this one time, it is much easier to do it again because it is a matter of simply updating numbers. Was this article meant to answering every question you have about landing sponsorships? Absolutely not. This is just the tip of the iceberg. But I have found that many singers and bands have little to no idea how to go about obtaining sponsorships. This article is meant to give those artists a basic plan and foundation for monetizing your shows and websites!

How to Get a Booking Agent

Rick Barker, Music Industry Blueprint's ### *"25 Minutes From Nashville"*

My goal has always been just to help as many people possible understand this crazy business. I always share with folks that we are trying to function in a dysfunctional business and, in most businesses, you do a job and get paid. Or you build a product and you get paid for that product. Or you work for an hour and you get paid for that hour.

The music business seems to be one of those that the rewards are not always in direct proportion to the work that you put in. That can be quite frustrating at times. One of the things that people have been bringing up a lot lately, especially at the live events that I do, is that people are really curious to know how to get a booking agent and how to get gigs. The first thing is you have to be able, in my opinion, to entertain. If you just sit there and play your songs, well, they can do that with their jukebox or a CD player. If you are going to entertain and bring something of value to the show, I think you stand a pretty good chance.

Booking agents get paid a percentage, usually 10%, of whatever it is they help the artist bring in. If they are calling a venue and they sell them a show for $5,000 dollars, that means the booking agent made $500 dollars and, in that, the booking agent has to do the contracts. There are a lot of things involved. They are not clearing a ton of cash in that situation.

So the booking agents are going to try to sign to their roster artists that generate income. It's very hard for them to have a roster full of a bunch of baby acts that are making only $200, $300, or $400 dollars a show. And a lot of you may be going, "Wow, I'd love to make that kind of money for a show." Well think about it.

If you book a $500 show, your booking agent only makes $50. It's going to be hard to pay your bills on 50- bucks. Major agencies, right now, they may see an act they like, they may see an act that is starting to get a buzz, they may see an act before they are getting ready to be signed to a record deal. And, at that point, remember we talked about the chart position goes up, the more you are able to play.

So don't feel bad when a major booking agent in the beginning stages of your career can't get you booked. And don't be shocked if you happen to get lucky and have a booking agent decide they would like to sign you to their roster and then get only a couple of shows in the beginning. They want to get you to sign because they are not the only booking agent in town. All of a sudden you have to sit and wait for a little while. Why? Well, when they call a venue, the venue is going to want to know what artist is available within their budget that has the most activity going on or has the best chance of putting butts in the seats.

If you are a brand new artist and you sound really good but you have no following, no online presence, nothing going on, you are not very attractive to them. No matter how great you sound, no matter how good you think your show is, if you don't have anything to bring to the table, why would the venue book you? And why would the booking agent risk that relationship by putting an act in there that they know can't sell tickets? A lot of times the booking agent's relationships will get you that first shot. And if a club owner took a chance on you, sent you and the booking agent $5,000 dollars and the club lost money that night because your show bombed, what's the chances of that club continuing to take a shot on new artists whenever that booking agent calls? Not good.

That's why the booking agents are being very selective. You have to understand that everybody wants them. Everything I teach, whether it be radio, trying to get a record deal, trying to get more gigs comes back to the same thing: build your audience first. If you bring something to the table, you will be turning down opportunities to perform. You will turn down offers from record companies. You will turn down offers from booking agents because, when you have something going on, everybody wants you.

So if you will take the time to do your own research, do your own booking, and you will do everything you can to make yourself a valuable commodity, you are going to have a much better shot of succeeding in this crazy, dysfunctional business that we absolutely love. First step is to become the best in your town. Every chance you get to play, play. Every chance you get to grab an email address, grab it. And once you master your town, branch out to the next 50-miles and go conquer that town. If it takes months then it takes months. And then branch out a little bit further and then branch out a little bit further.

Handle your state and the surrounding states and consistently put butts in the seats, consistently sell your shows, consistently sell merchandise. That is when you will have a story to take to a booking agent and say, "I grossed 200-thousand dollars last year on my own. Imagine what happens if I get someone like you behind me," and the booking agent sits there going, "Okay, wait a minute..." Even if you just duplicate that 200-thousand, at least the booking agent's made 20-thousand.

Now you may be saying to yourself, "Why would I go get a booking agent and just give him 20-thousand dollars?" Because now that booking agent can go and tell your story to HIS bosses and may be able get you opening dates on bigger tours. You have to remember to look for the big picture. Don't worry about what you might have to spend or invest or give up in the beginning. If you are in it for the long haul, and if you are in it for the big picture, you have to keep in mind that relationships cost money and expertise cost money.

I can guarantee you that most of the shows you have done, you weren't running through the legal contracts that these booking agents are going through. That costs money. So, go out, conquer your state, conquer the states around you, and then start walking into these booking agents' offices showing them what you have done instead of what you think you could do if just given a chance. They've heard that story over and over and over again.

CHAPTER 8

Health Concern

The Hidden Dangers of the Sound of Music

Wade Sutton, Rocket to the Stars

The damage to your hearing caused by loud music at your show this weekend will not rear its ugly head until nearly ten years from now.

Think about that for a moment.

I remember exactly where I was the first time I heard that fact. It was just a few days after Memorial Day in 2012. Rocket to the Stars' massive singing competition was in full swing and we were about six weeks away from our finals. Many of us from the show were gathered in an upstairs room at CJ Cochran's Day Spa and Salon about an hour north of Pittsburgh, Pennsylvania and it was the first time we invited doctors from the University of Pittsburgh Medical Center to talk to our contestants about hearing loss prevention and vocal health.

Read that statement again and let it sink in: "The damage to your hearing caused by loud music at your show this weekend will not rear its ugly head until nearly ten years from now."

Meet Dr. Catherine V. Palmer, PhD...

Dr. Catherine V. Palmer, PhD is one of my favorite people that I have met since founding Rocket to the Stars. She was hired at the University of Pittsburgh Medical Center in 1990 and became director of Audiology and Hearing Aids in the Department of Otolaryngology in 1998. Her education is impressive, having earned her undergraduate degree from the University of Massachusetts at Amherst before receiving her master's degree and doctorate at Northwestern University. Dr. Palmer's biography on the UPMC website says she specializes in rehabilitative audiology including "the use of hearing aids and other assistive devices to improve communications for individuals with hearing loss." She created, and has since directed, the Musician's Hearing Center at UPMC in 2003. It goes without saying that she really knows her stuff... and she has been a very good friend to Rocket to the Stars over the past two years. She was the first person I called when I decided to write this article.

One of my previous interviews with Dr. Palmer came in the form of a thirty-minute radio segment that was recorded a little more than one year ago. During that discussion, Dr. Palmer brought up the fact that, for many years, many musicians and singers refused to wear hearing protection because the earplugs that were available at the time attenuated some sounds more than others. It resulted in the muffling of speech and music, something artists simply would not tolerate. Unfortunately for many of them, from the heavy metal guitarists shredding in sold out arenas to the trombone player in the high school music class, they did not realize just what they were exposing themselves to.

What happens when you suffer hearing loss...

To understand what happens when you lose your hearing, you must first have a working knowledge of HOW you hear. The ear is made of up three major areas: outer ear, middle ear, and inner ear. When sound waves travel through the outer ear, they cause the eardrum to vibrate. The eardrum works in partnership with three small bones in the middle ear to amplify those vibrations as they make their way to the inner ear. It is there that the vibrations pass through the fluid contained within the cochlea.

Got all that? There is a little more to it, so stick with me. The cochlea has nerve cells. Attached to those nerve cells are thousands of tiny hairs (cilia). Those hairs take the sound vibrations and turn them into electrical signals that are sent to your brain, resulting in you hearing what you hear.

Hearing loss can be caused by a number of things but for the purpose of this article, we are concentrating on hearing loss brought on by loud music. When you are exposed to prolonged periods of loud noise or music, the hairs and nerves in the cochlea (in the inner ear) suffer wear and tear. That results in the electrical signals to your brain not being transmitted properly. The hearing loss leaves musicians and singers having problems with background noise mixing with words.

And another thing to consider: www.mayoclinic.com says heredity can make you more prone to that type of hearing loss. Another thing to keep in mind is that loud, sustained noises aren't the only thing putting you at risk. Sudden blasts of sound are also dangerous as they could result in a ruptured eardrum, known as tympanic membrane perforation. It is similar to when somebody experiences sudden changes in pressure.

When loud becomes too loud...

Dr. Palmer gave me some interesting numbers (see chart below) compiled by the Center for Human Performance and Health in Ontario, Canada. It shows measurements of decibel levels dB (A)) of various musical instruments and bands. Below that are additional figures I found on NoiseHelp.com while writing this story. Many doctors say the 90 dB (A) level is when you start putting yourself at serious risk of hearing damage. Many people will find it hard to believe, but studies show a flute can reach decibel levels comparable to a jackhammer, while an orchestra peaking during a performance can be almost as loud as a jet engine during take off. Even something as small as a violin can easily go beyond that

90 dB (A) mark... and that is an instrument that typically rests just a few short inches from the musician's ear.

Musical Instrument Sound Levels

Normal piano practice	60-70 dB(A)
Chamber Music in Small Auditorium	75-85 dB(A)
Piano Fortissimo	92-95 dB(A)
Violin	84-103 dB(A)
Cello	82-92 dB(A)
Oboe	90-94 dB(A)
Flute	85-111 dB(A)
Piccolo	95-112 dB(A)
Clarinet	92-103 dB(A)
French Horn	90-106 dB(A)
Trombone	85-114 dB(A)
Band (average)	97 dB(A)
Timpani and Bass Drum Rolls	106 dB(A)
Orchestra Peaks	120-137 dB(A)
Band at a Sporting Event	100-120 dB(A)

Additional Common Sound Levels

Jackhammer	110 dB(A)
Emergency Vehicle Siren	115 dB(A)
Air Raid Siren	135 dB(A)
Jet Engine During Take Off	140 dB(A)

Another thing that jumps out to me when looking at the numbers Dr. Palmer sent to Rocket to the Stars for this piece: a band performing at a sporting event typically registers between 100 - 120 dB(A). Note that the range provided there is for just the band while it is performing and does not take into account noise generated by screaming fans and stadium public address systems, which are loud in their own right. In fact those can easily hit the 100-decibel mark and, in that situation, you are exposed to those loud noises over a period of three or four hours.

Another common hearing problem for singers and musicians...

Another common problem many singers and musicians find themselves coping with is called tinnitus. That is the extremely annoying ringing, buzzing, clicking, or hissing you get in your ears. The Mayo Clinic says tinnitus isn't a condition itself - it is more a symptom of an underlying condition, such as age-related hearing loss, an ear injury, or a circulatory system disorder.

There are two types of tinnitus. Subjective tinnitus causes ringing and hissing that only you can hear. The other type, objective tinnitus, is a form of tinnitus that your doctor can hear during an examination. Objective tinnitus is rare and Mayo Clinic says it can be caused by a blood vessel problem, muscle contractions, or an inner ear bone condition. Tinnitus has several risk factors that go beyond exposure to loud music. Smokers have a higher risk of developing it and men are more likely to experience it than women.

Tinnitus brings many concerns other than the "phantom" noises that annoy you while coping with it. Doctors say it can have a significant effect on your quality of life, leading to problems such as fatigue, stress, and sleep problems, anxiety, and depression. If you find yourself coping with tinnitus, don't ignore it because it can be treated. Some musicians and singers try to live in denial thinking the problem is more serious than it really is and, as a result, they don't seek help even though it is available. Dr. Palmer says the treatment program at UPMC usually takes 12 to 18 months to complete.

Protect yourself before you wreck yourself...

One of the best forms of ear protection on the market, not to mention they are inexpensive, are the ER20s by Etymotic Research. The standard fit plugs can be purchased on Amazon.com for less than $20.00 USD (at the time of this writing). Dr. Palmer and the rest of the folks at the University of Pittsburgh Medical Center recommend them and they have high user ratings on Amazon. In fact,

Dr. Palmer loves these little guys so much she talks about them when she goes into Pittsburgh-area high schools as part of a program to educate bands on hearing loss.

Why do musicians and singers think so highly of them? Because they reduce the decibel level of sound going into your ear without making what you hear sound muffled. The sound quality is preserved while protecting your hearing. Look into them or something comparable.

✎ WRAP-UP / CONTACT US

So there you have it! Rick and Wade hope this book has provided you with some food for thought. Both of them would love to hear your feedback and are more than willing to answer your questions and assist you in your pursuit of a career in music.

Rick can be contacted via e-mail at Rick@RickBarker.com. Be sure to check out his FREE video series at www.MusicIndustry-Blueprint.com! The videos are packed with information vital to singers, musicians, and bands trying to make a living off their music.

You can e-mail Wade at WadeSutton@RockettotheStars.com. Not only does his website, www.RockettotheStars.com, offer a lot of free content that is priceless for artists, you can also subscribe to his e-mail list for exclusive discounts for his services and online classes...and find out how to schedule a FREE preliminary consultation (for a limited time only and spaces are limited)!

Do NOT be afraid to pursue a career in commercial music. Do NOT be intimidated by what you have to learn to be successful. EDUCATE yourself to give yourself the best chance at making it. Like Rick always says:

"You don't drown by falling into water. You drown by staying there."

It's time to either get out of the water, or learn to swim!

Made in the USA
Las Vegas, NV
16 January 2021